One Flesh

One Flesh

*A Biblical Perspective
on the Permanence of Marriage*

JOE FOGLE

Wipf & Stock
PUBLISHERS
Eugene, Oregon

ONE FLESH
A Biblical Perspective on the Permanence of Marriage

ISBN 13: 978-1-4982-4959-1

Unless otherwise indicated, all Scripture quotations are from the authorized Version of the Bible.

To my wife Brenda,
whose encouragement and patience
show Christ's love in our marriage.

~~~~~~~

The first martyr recorded in
the New Testament was killed
for speaking against the sin of
divorce and remarriage.

A Note to the Reader

Throughout this manuscript reference has been made to Hebrew and Greek words. They have been transliterated into an English equivalent in order to give the reader a greater understanding of the grammar and syntax involved. Each word is then coded according to Strong's numbering system so that the reader can reference the word for himself.

For example, the English word fornication is transliterated from the original Greek as *porneia*. Strong's number is then given which is 4202. It is hoped that this information will be profitable to the reader.

Contents

Introduction

THE IMPORTANCE of the subject of divorce and remarriage and its relationship to the biblical context is two fold:

First, divorce is a destructive force upon individual families as well as society in general. The divorce and remarriage rate has not only risen in western society but it has increased dramatically in the evangelical church over the last fifty years. Before this divorce did take place in evangelical Christian households but they were a small percentage when compared to the number of marriages in the evangelical community at large. Those that did occur were usually discouraged or frowned upon by most evangelical groups.

In recent decades divorce and remarriage has become an acceptable alternative to a life long monogamous commitment. In some cases it is not only condoned but even encouraged. It is interesting that something that is so destructive to both the family unit and society in general is both allowed and sometimes encouraged by the evangelical Christian community. It is most tragic when young children are involved. They are told by those in spiritual authority that it is okay if mommy and daddy get divorced and marry someone else. The child is then led to believe that this traumatic event which has brought both turmoil and insecurity into his or her life is some how condoned by a loving God.

Second, and probably the most important issue regarding the subject of divorce and remarriage is that of sinning against a holy and righteous God. The Bible states that divorce and remarriage is adultery. Even those who claim an exception will have to admit that any divorce and remarriage that takes place outside of the so called *exception clause* is still considered adultery. Adultery is a serious charge. The Bible sternly warns Christians to flee sexual immorality and ensure that the marriage bed remains undefiled. God will judge both fornicators and adulterers (Heb. 13:4).

Since judgment awaits those who commit sexual sin it would seem wise that Christians should understand just what may be included in the definition of sexual sin. One of the purposes of this manuscript is to determine whether divorce and remarriage is considered a sexual sin by the God of the Bible. It is fully understood that my conclusions are a minority opinion in the evangelical church today. This is not a deterrent. There have been times in the history of God's people, both with Israel and the church, where the majority have been wrong. If I am incorrect and divorce and remarriage is acceptable to God then I will be judged as an incorrect teacher of God's word. If I am correct that divorce and remarriage is not acceptable to God then judgment may await those involved.

This work is titled "One Flesh" because the Scriptures teach that marriage is a lifelong *one flesh* covenant relationship. It is this *one flesh* union that joins the couple until death do they part. This is the basis for the teaching that remarriage after divorce is considered adultery.

It is often more important to know why a person believes what they do than what they believe. The reason why it is believed that marriage is permanent is because of the *one flesh* bond. Those who believe that divorce and remarriage is allowed must of necessity believe one of two things. Either they believe that the one flesh bond does not exist in the first place or they believe that at some point after the two become flesh the one flesh bond may cease to exist. Both are logically flawed positions that break down under careful scrutiny.

The motives for presenting the evidence are twofold. First, if Christians teach the permanence of the marriage relationship perhaps it may encourage some to remain committed to their marriage and work on issues when they arise rather than seeking divorce. Second, it may deter some from divorcing and remarrying if they know that their actions are not pleasing to God and the potential for judgment exists. Ten years of research on this subject are presented in the following pages. Please read on.

Chapter 1

The Old Testament

Genesis 1 and 2

So God created man in His own image, in the image of God created He him; male and female created He them. (Gen. 1:27)

And Adam said, This is now bone of my bones, and flesh of my flesh: she shall be called Woman, because she was taken out of Man. Therefore shall a man leave his father and his mother, and shall cleave unto his wife: and they shall be one flesh. (Gen. 2:23–24)

MARRIAGE WAS ordained to be a *one flesh* covenant relationship. Adam and Eve were literally "one flesh." This is because Eve was formed from the physical flesh and bone of Adam's side. From this time on their descendants were to marry and be joined in one flesh unions. Divorce was not part of God's original plan. Even after the fall God had no plan for Adam and Eve or their descendants to divorce and remarry. Divorce was an invention of man brought on by the hardness of man's heart.

It is possible that *one flesh* also has a predictive sense to it. Those who marry will normally produce offspring. The children they produce are literally *one flesh* brought forth by two parents. Children are a constant reminder that two became one flesh.

Genesis 2:24 states: Man was to "leave" (*azab*/5800) his father and mother. Man was to "cleave" (*dabaq*/1692) to his wife. Man will be "one flesh" (*basar*/1320) with his wife. Cleave means to cling, stick to, or be joined together with. Cleave is a covenant term also used to show God's relationship to His people (cf. Deut. 10:20, 11:22, 13:4, 30:20; Josh 22:5, 23:8; Ruth 1:14–16). The phrase "one flesh" carries a similar idea to that of being kin or blood relatives.

To refer to someone as being "bone of my bones, and flesh of my flesh" (Gen. 2:23) was to say more than they shared the same bodily heritage. To say that a man and woman become one flesh is to say more than they are united bodily. It expresses the oneness that they share because of God joining them together. The kinship nature of marriage is also indicated by the formula "bone of my bone, and flesh of my flesh" (cf. Gen. 29:14, 37:27; Judg. 9:2; 2 Sam. 5:1, 19:12,13; I Chr. 11:1).

Throughout the Old Testament marriage is called a covenant (*berith*/1285). Proverbs 2:17 mentions the adulterous wife who forsakes the companion of her youth and in doing so forsakes the covenant that she made before God.

The marriage covenant is more than a bilateral covenant between two people. It includes God as a third party who joins the man and the woman in a covenant commitment. Malachi 2:14 speaks of God being a witness to this covenant between husband and wife. This is why Jesus could legitimately state "What therefore God has joined together, let no man separate" (Mark 10:9).

The nature of this *one flesh* covenant is indissoluble. A husband and wife may sin against one another but nothing except death or the rapture can cause them to cease being husband and wife. This is why marriage is used as a picture of God's relationship with Israel in the Old Testament. Some claim that since some covenants are conditional and therefore dissoluble then the marriage covenant is also conditional and dissoluble. The issue is not whether some covenants are dissoluble but whether the one flesh marriage covenant is dissoluble. The evidence points to a consummated marriage being an indissoluble covenant. It is for this reason that some who approach the subject of divorce and remarriage deny the covenant nature of marriage or ignore the subject altogether. A common misconception is that marriage is a contract that may be broken similar to any other legal contract.

This conclusion is often supported by the claim that certain ancient near eastern marriage covenants included contractual stipulations that allowed spouses to divorce and remarry for various reasons. Since some of these covenants resemble modern day marriage contracts then divorce and remarriage is to be allowed under certain circumstances. The main problem with this type of reasoning is that the biblical covenant of marriage is not based upon ancient near eastern cultural practices. It is based upon the one flesh covenant established by God between Adam and Eve in the Garden of Eden.

When God brought Adam and Eve together as husband and wife there were no contractual obligations listed. They were not given a list of stipulations wherein if one party breached the contract the marriage could end in divorce. Contractual marriages did exist in ancient near eastern cultures but these were stipulations invented and established by men. Applying these types of contractual stipulations to the modern application of biblical texts on divorce and remarriage is a type of reverse exegesis.[1] It is invalid to study the actions of man and then claim they are not only condoned by God but form the basis for God's will concerning the permanence of marriage. This reasoning was invalidated by Jesus Himself. The Pharisees wanted to debate the ancient near eastern divorce and remarriage practices which occurred during the time of Moses. Jesus refused to enter into their debate and took them back to the beginning of creation where God established the two as one flesh (Matt. 19:5).

Deuteronomy 24

By this time in history, divorce and remarriage were practiced by the Israelites. This was not God's design for marriage it was a traditional custom invented by man. God intervened and prohibited the practice of a second remarriage back to one's original spouse.

The Jews allowed the man, not the woman, the right to initiate divorce for "some uncleanness" (*ervat*/6172; *dabar*/1697). Literally this means a "naked" or "indecent" thing. By the time of Christ the Jews had misinterpreted this phrase to mean everything from adultery to burning a meal. "Some Indecency" does not refer to adultery. The penalty for this was death. It also would not refer to those who had sexual relations during the betrothal period. This was also punished by stoning (Deut. 22:20–24). Some believe that "some indecency" may refer to a physical deformity in the woman. Others believe that it may refer to her inability to bear children. The precise meaning of the term is no longer clear.

Some believe that Deuteronomy 24:1–4 established or gave approval for divorce and remarriage. A careful exegesis of the text does not produce this conclusion.

> When a man takes a wife and marries her, and it happens that she finds no favor in his eyes because he has found some indecency in her, and he writes her a certificate of divorce, puts it in her hand, and sends her out of his house, When she has departed from his house, and goes and becomes another man's wife, if the latter husband detests her and writes her a certificate of divorce, puts it in her hand, and sends her out of his house, or if the latter husband dies who took her to be his wife, then her former husband who

---

1. David Instone-Brewer, *Divorce and Remarriage*, p. 15.

divorced her must not take her back to be his wife after she has been defiled; for this is an abomination before the Lord, and you shall not bring sin on the land which the Lord your God is giving you as an inheritance. (Deut. 24:1–4)

The text states that divorce was happening because a man found some indecency in his wife. It says she went and became another man's wife. The text does not say God approved of this. It is possible that this was happening numerous times to the same woman (Deut. 24:3).

There is only one piece of legislation in this passage, it is contained in verse 4. The first three verses form the *protasis* which specifies the conditions that must apply for the implementation of the legislation. Verse 4 contains the *apodosis* which expresses the consequence of the legislation.

At this point in history the Law did not regulate the first, second, or subsequent divorces. It only regulated remarriage in one case; the remarriage of a woman back to her original husband.

Keil and Delitzsch write:

> In these verses, however, divorce is not established as a right; all that is done is, that in case of a divorce a reunion with the divorced wife is forbidden, if in the meantime she had married another man, even though the second husband had also put her away, or had died.[2]

This law was given to protect the rights of the woman. If a man could divorce his wife and then take her back this would encourage frivolous divorces and open the door for covert adultery. The law concerning divorce would prevent her from being used in this way.

This law may also have been given to protect the rights and dowry of the woman. The text mentions the common cultural practices of that day. In Deuteronomy 24:1, the first wife had failed in her marital duties (done something "indecent") which caused the husband to divorce her. Because of this the husband would have been allowed to retain her dowry and any material assets she may have acquired during the marriage. She was sent out with nothing but her apparel. This led to the practice of women placing coins in their headgear and wearing large amounts of jewelry. This would give them some financial resources if they were divorced.

In Deuteronomy 24:3, the second divorce, the woman's conduct is not questioned. The text states that the man "turns against" or "hates" her. He then divorces her and sends her from his house. Under the custom of that day the woman was entitled to the return of her dowry, was allowed

---

2. Keil and Delitzsch, *The Fifth Book of Moses*, p. 416.

to retain her material assets, and could potentially be compensated financially as part of the divorce settlement. In the case of the husband's death she could receive a portion of her husband's estate.

The first husband is prohibited from remarrying her because he would benefit from unjust financial gain. The first husband had put away his wife because of "some indecency." He had divorced her, retained all of her material assets, and sent her away with nothing but her apparel. She went out, remarried, and acquired other material assets. The first husband could now claim that she was not indecent and be financially rewarded by remarrying her and once again taking control of her material assets. This would be a form of stealing.[3]

In modern legal terms this is estoppel. Estoppel prevents a person from asserting a fact or a claim that is inconsistent with a position he previously took. As applied to Deuteronomy 24 the first husband claimed that he found "some indecency" (*ervat dabar*) in her. This is why he divorced her. Now he seeks to remarry her and would of necessity need to claim that he finds no "indecency" in her. These are contradictory claims both used to his benefit. He benefited in the original divorce her by claiming she was "indecent." Now he seeks to benefit again by claiming she is not "indecent."

Verse 4 gives the only regulations of the text. The woman who was divorced and remarried was forever prohibited from returning to her original husband, even if her second husband died. Two reasons are given for this restriction. First, she had been "defiled" (*tamel*2930). This word can be translated as "cultically unclean" or "to pollute oneself." It is the same word used throughout the Old Testament regarding a person who has sexual relations that are prohibited. These included rape (Gen. 34:5); incest (Lev. 18:5–18); adultery (Lev. 18:20); homosexuality (Lev. 18:22); and bestiality (Lev. 18:23). The evidence points to it being remarriage that defiled the woman and made her unclean. Second, the practice of returning to one's original husband, after divorce and remarriage, is an abomination to God and brings sin upon the land.

Craigie writes:

> The language (*defiled*) suggests adultery (see Lev. 18:20). The sense is that the woman's remarriage after the first divorce is similar to adultery in that the woman cohabits with another man. However, if the woman were then to remarry her first husband, after divorcing the second, the analogy with adultery would become even

3. Raymond Westbrook, *Prohibition of Restoration of Marriage in Deuteronomy 24:1–14*.

more complete; the woman lives first with one man, then another, and finally returns to the first. Thus the intent of the legislation seems to be to apply certain restrictions on the already existing practice of divorce. If divorce became too easy, then it could be abused and it would become a "legal" form of committing adultery. The legislation thus restricts what may have been a loophole in the older custom. The purpose of the restriction is to keep free from sin the land which God would soon be giving to his people as an inheritance.[4]

Deuteronomy 24:1–4 did not establish divorce. It did not give Divine approval for divorce or remarriage. The only command or regulation given, was the prohibition of the divorced and remarried woman from ever returning to a conjugal relationship with her original husband.

The civil legislation of Moses did not deal directly with the traditional customs of polygamy, concubinage, or divorce. This does not mean God approved of them. The civil legislation was based on moral law, yet it was a practical regulation for the people. It did not deal with all possible matters, nor did it absolutely prohibit all social evils, because, as Jesus said, "their hearts were hard."

Modern defenders of the right to divorce and remarriage seek to engage others in debate over the meaning of "some indecency" in this passage. Like the Pharisees of Jesus' day they seek to find legal loopholes to justify divorce and remarriage. The Lord Jesus Christ did not enter into a debate over the meaning of "some indecency." Instead, He took them back to God's original divine plan for marriage at the beginning of creation. Christians should base their view of divorce and remarriage on the Genesis account and the words of Jesus in the Gospels.

The Nature of God's Covenant

Many of the Reformers resorted to the use of interpretive legal fiction to allow Christians to divorce and remarry. Since the Mosaic Law sanctioned the death penalty against an adulterous spouse, the New Testament Christian could now see their adulterous spouse as figuratively dead. They were then free to divorce and remarry. I do not know of any modern writers who currently hold this view. Instead they have taken another route to allow divorce and remarriage. They claim God divorced Israel, therefore the believer is also free to divorce their adulterous spouse and remarry. At the outset it needs to be stressed that the doctrine of *divorce* and remar-

4 Peter Craigie, *Deuteronomy*, p. 305.

riage is to be grounded in exegesis of relevant New Testament passages. Nevertheless, since this argument is used by current writers, we will look at what the Old Testament has to say about God's covenant relationship with Israel.

Did God completely forsake Israel so that she had no future hope of restoration? God disciplined Israel for disobedience, but did He put her away and take another nation to be His wife? For modern expositors to claim God's relationship with Israel allows Christians to divorce and remarry, these questions must be answered in the affirmative.

The Abrahamic Covenant

The beginning point for the Jewish nation took place with the call of Abraham. Before this time in history there were no chosen people. Individuals trusted in the living God but Yahweh had not yet called any particular nation. In Genesis 12 God called Abraham and promised to make him a great nation. God made three unconditional promises to Abraham. 1) He promised him *land.* 2) He promised him a *seed.* 3) He promised to make him a *blessing.*

> Now the Lord said to Abram, Get thee out of thy country, and from thy kindred, and from thy father's house, unto a land that I will show thee: And I will make of thee a great nation, and I will bless thee, and make thy name great; and thou shalt be a blessing: And I will bless them that bless thee, and curse him that curseth thee: and in thee shall all the families of the earth be blessed. (Gen. 12:1–3)

Is this covenant conditional or unconditional? Genesis 17:7, 13, and 19; First Chronicles 16:16–17; and Psalm 105:9–10 all claim this covenant is eternal. It is based on the sovereign choice and promise of God. If a covenant is eternal, then it can not be conditional.

O. T. Allis writes this about the covenant:

> It is true that, in the express terms of the covenant with Abraham, obedience is not stated as a condition.[5]

If the covenant was unconditional at its inception, it remains such through out history. Galatians 3:15 states that the Abrahamic covenant cannot be altered.

---

5 O. T. Allis, *Prophecy and the Church*, p. 33.

> Brethren, I speak after the manner of men; Though it be a man's covenant, yet if it be confirmed, no man disannulleth, or addeth thereto. (Gal. 3:15)

In Genesis 15:17 God passed through the cut animals to confirm what He had previously promised. The fact that God alone passed through the sacrifice, emphasizes that the promise was unilateral and therefore unconditional.

Later in Genesis 17:9–14 God gave Abraham the rite of circumcision as an outward visible sign of the covenant. This rite was a personal act that related each male to the covenant but had nothing to do with the unconditional nature of it. Women could not be circumcised, yet became partakers of the covenant. One uncircumcised man could not annul the covenant for the rest of the nation any more than one unbeliever can void the grace of God for everyone else.

The covenant was reiterated and confirmed to Isaac and Jacob after disobedience on the part of each. Certain blessings may be attached to unconditional covenants which may require some response from each individual in order to receive personal benefit but the integrity of an unconditional covenant remains intact whether an individual remains loyal or not. There may be delays, postponements, and chastisements but an eternal unconditional covenant cannot be broken. If a covenant is unconditional at its inception, it remains so through out history. Since God chose Abraham's seed to always be a nation before Him, He will never *permanently* put Israel away and marry another nation. Out of the Abrahamic covenant came three more covenants: Palestinian (*land*), Davidic (*seed*), and New (*blessing*) Covenants.

The Palestinian and Mosaic Covenants

The Palestinian covenant is found in Deuteronomy 30:1–10. It was given in fulfillment of the land promises made to Abraham, Isaac, and Jacob. Ezekiel 16:60 calls it an eternal covenant because it is an amplification of the unconditional Abrahamic covenant. It was given because God knew the people would break the law. This was a reminder that God would never completely forsake the nation of Israel. The Mosaic covenant is given in Exodus 19 and Deuteronomy 28. It was conditional and based on the people's obedience. If the people obeyed, they would be blessed. If the people disobeyed, they would be cursed. Most conservative scholars place the date of Abraham around 2100 BC. Moses received the Law around 1440 BC. In the 600–700 years between the Abrahamic and Mosaic covenants there were many opportunities for God to cut off the seed of Abraham for their sinful behavior. Nevertheless, the unconditional promise of God stood firm. God chose Israel in an unmerited act of gracious favor. Obedience to the Mosaic covenant did not decide who the people of God would be. It did not decide whether they would retain their status as a chosen nation. These were decided centuries before through the sovereign choice of God. Obedience to the law decided if Israel would be cursed or blessed.

The Mosaic covenant anticipated the disobedience and subsequent dispersions of Israel under the Assyrians (722 BC), Babylonians (586 BC), and Romans (AD 70). The Palestinian covenant assured Israel that when these calamities were over, they would repent and God would restore the people. Israel would once again possess the land. This is a frequent theme of the prophets (Jer. 30:3; Joel 3:1). This will ultimately be fulfilled at the second advent of Messiah, before the beginning of the millennial kingdom. The unconditional Abrahamic and Palestinian covenants are in no way abrogated by the temporal and conditional Mosaic covenant.

The Davidic Covenant

The Davidic covenant is the *seed* part of the Abrahamic covenant (2 Sam. 7:12–16). It was made while the Mosaic Law was in effect. God promised three things to David. First, David would have a son. Second, David's lineage would be established forever. Third, David's throne and earthly political kingdom would be established over Israel forever. God promised similar things to Solomon. God promised Solomon he would build the temple. He also promised that the throne would remain forever. He did not promise Solomon that his seed would always be on the throne. This is important because Solomon's line was cut off because of disobedience. First Kings 9:6–7 makes it clear that God would cut off Solomon or his sons if they turned away from God. David's line would continue as God promised.

In accordance with the Word of God, Jesus the Messiah did come from the line of David. The final fulfillment of this covenant will be a future literal reign of Christ on the throne of David in Jerusalem (cf. Rev. 20:6). God seems to have anticipated the arguments, that disobedience abrogates unconditional covenants. Disobedience brought punishment to Solomon and his sons. Disobedience brought death to David's first son through Bathsheba. Disobedience brought the sword of the Angel of the Lord on the people for David's census. Disobedience has currently interrupted the reign of David's seed on the throne. Disobedience *does not* nullify God's covenant with His people. An important thing to realize is that *God made his covenant with David before David committed adultery with Bathsheba.* If adultery or any other sin could break God's covenant, then why wasn't this accomplished by David's sin? The answer is simple. Sin does not, and can not, nullify an unconditional covenant created by God.

The New Covenant

In Jeremiah 31:31–37 God made a new covenant with the nation of Israel. He claimed that they had broken the conditional Mosaic covenant, but His "unconditional love" (*chesed*/2617) wouldn't give up on them. The new covenant is an extension of the blessing part of the Abrahamic covenant. It is based on unconditional grace resting on the "I will" of God. The new covenant is everlasting and promises impartation of a renewed mind and heart. It promises Israel that her sins will be forgiven and that God will never forsake them.

> Thus saith the Lord, who gives the sun for a light by day, and the ordinances of the moon and of the stars by night, who divides the sea when the waves thereof roar; The Lord of hosts is his name: If those ordinances depart from before me, saith the Lord, then the seed of Israel also shall cease from being a nation before me forever. Thus saith the Lord; If heaven above can be measured, and the foundations of the earth searched out beneath, I will also cast off all the seed of Israel for all they have done, saith the Lord. (Jer. 31:35–37)

God uses the unsearchableness of the universe and the foundations of the earth as proof that He will never completely cast off Israel as His chosen nation. This in spite of the fact that they broke the Mosaic Law.

Was God Divorced and Remarried?

Some have surmised that since God claims to have divorced Israel, then divorce is allowed for the Christian also. In response to this, it must be reiterated that New Testament doctrine is to be built on New Testament passages that specifically speak on this subject. Doctrine can be rooted in the Old Testament, as Jesus did by quoting from Genesis chapters 1 and 2. It is not to be built on Old Testament metaphors or analogies which use similar terms, but do not speak directly to the subject.

We have shown the permanent relationship God has with Israel. With this foundation laid, we'll look at some verses which interpreters use to allow Christians to divorce and remarry.

Isaiah 50:1

> Thus saith the Lord, Where is the bill of your mother's divorcement, whom I have put away? or which of my creditors is it to whom I have sold you? Behold, for your iniquities have ye sold yourselves, and for your transgressions is your mother put away. (Isa. 50:1)

God called Abraham *circa* 2100 BC. The Mosaic covenant had been in effect since 1440 BC. The book of Isaiah was penned *circa* 700 BC. The seed of Abraham had been a chosen people for 1400 years. They had lived under the Mosaic Law for 700 years. They had sinned many times during this period, but they were still God's chosen people. This passage speaks of God divorcing His people, but it also speaks of Him selling them to creditors. These are figures of speech that are used to show God's punishment and discipline of His children. There is nothing mentioned in this passage of them ceasing to be the *wife* of God. The basic theme of chapters 40–66 is comfort and salvation for the nation of Israel. They must undergo discipline for their sin, but God will restore them. The furthest Isaiah 50:1 could be taken is that the adulterous wife could temporarily be put away for her sin, yet she doesn't cease being a wife. Even this would be stretching New Testament doctrine since husbands are commanded to love their wives as Christ loved the Church. Christ disciplines His church, but He never divorces them. Notice this passage also says Israel was sold to creditors. The Jews bought and sold women like chattel. If taken in the same literal manner, then a man could sell his wife to creditors. Isaiah 54:4 speaks of Israel being a widow. Did God actually die? If taken literally, we wouldn't know if Israel was widowed or divorced. The basic meaning of this passage is that God allowed Israel to be temporarily chastised for her sins. When taken as a whole, the book of Isaiah is filled with other verses that show God's steadfast and forgiving love to Israel.

Isaiah 54:5–10 has this beautiful passage that sums up God's relationship to Israel:

> For thy maker is thine husband, The Lord of hosts is His name; And thy redeemer the Holy One of Israel; the God of the whole earth shall He be called. For the Lord hath called thee as a woman

forsaken and grieved in spirit, and a wife of youth, when thou wast refused, saith thy God. For a small moment I have forsaken thee, but with great mercies I will gather thee. In a little wrath I hid my face from thee for a moment: But with everlasting kindness I will have mercy on thee, saith the Lord thy redeemer. For this is as the waters of Noah unto me; for as I have sworn that the waters of Noah should no more go over the earth, so I have sworn that I would not be wroth with thee nor rebuke thee. For the mountains shall depart and the hills be removed, but my kindness shall not depart from thee, neither shall the covenant of my peace be removed, saith the Lord that hath mercy on thee. (Isa. 54:5–10)

Notice that this passage comes *after* the passage used by people to allow for divorce and remarriage. God still claimed to be Israel's husband. His wrath lasts only a moment, but His mercy is forever. The mountains and the hills will pass away before God will break His covenant with Israel.

Jeremiah 3:8

And I saw, when for all the causes whereby backsliding Israel committed adultery I had put her away, and given her a bill of divorce; yet her treacherous sister Judah feared not, but went and played the harlot also (Jer. 3:8).

Jeremiah chapter 3 was written *circa* 625 BC. Israel went into captivity for her sin and it was to be a warning and call to repentance for the southern kingdom of Judah. Some have used this verse to prove divorce and remarriage is appropriate under certain circumstances. Israel had not committed literal but spiritual adultery. Jeremiah 3:9 makes it clear that her adultery was with stones and trees, meaning idolatry. If consistency is applied, this kind of interpretation would allow a man to divorce a wife who had committed spiritual apostasy. The point of the entire passage is that Israel was the treacherous one. God was faithful and was beckoning Israel to return. Not a word is mentioned about God remarrying another nation after the divorce. God claims the Mosaic Law does not allow the divorced and remarried woman to return (Jer. 3:1) yet God allowed Israel to return in direct violation of Deuteronomy 24:1–4. When rules of normative interpretation are taken away, (as some have conveniently done), Scripture can be made to say whatever one wants it to say. God claims to have married Judah as well as her sister Israel. This would be in violation of Leviticus 18:18. If a Christian can use this verse to divorce his wife and remarry, then it would be just as valid, (using this interpretive method), to allow polygamy. All this proves is that Old Testament metaphors shouldn't be stretched to teach New Testament doctrine.

Hosea 1 and 2

> Then said God, Call his name Lo-ammi: for ye are not my people, and I will not be your God. Yet the number of the children of Israel shall be as the sand of the sea, which cannot be measured nor numbered; and it will come to pass, that in the place where it is said unto them, Ye are not my people, there it shall be said unto them, Ye are the sons of the living God. (Hos. 1:9–10)

> Plead with your mother, plead: for she is not my wife, neither am I her husband: Let her therefore put away her whoredoms out of her sight, and her adulteries from between her breasts; Lest I strip her naked, and set her as in the day that she was born, and make her as a wilderness, and set her like a dry land, and slay her with thirst. (Hos. 2:2–3)

Hosea's ministry took place preceding and following Israel's captivity (722 BC). Hosea was a divine messenger to warn Israel that her apostasy would bring the curses of God as promised in Deuteronomy 28:15–68. A cursory reading of Hosea will show that one main theme of the book is to show God's forgiveness to a sinful people. Rather than giving up on Israel, God used Hosea's marriage to a harlot to illustrate His steadfast unceasing love. Though God did claim to have divorced Israel, the entire picture must be kept in perspective. Israel had broken the conditional Mosaic covenant yet they still had the unconditional Abrahamic covenant as proof that they would always be the people of God. The fact that God disciplined Israel proves that they still were His chosen people.

Amazingly enough, some expositors use these very Scriptures to try to prove that Christians have a right to divorce and remarry. They completely overlook that Hosea 1:9 is temporal, yet verses 10–11 give the final condition. Namely, in this same place Israel and Judah will be called sons of the living God. *Lo-ammi* (not my people) is used as an analogy for God's discipline of Israel. It cannot be stretched to say that God permanently put away Israel. It cannot be used to prove a divorced person ever has a right to remarry. In Hosea 2:2 the word adultery is used as a metaphor for spiritual apostasy. Hosea 2:3 claims God will strip Israel naked and cause her to die of dehydration in the desert. Are Christians to punish adulterous wives in this manner?

The permanence of Israel's relationship is rooted in the unconditional Abrahamic covenant. Their discipline, captivities, and *divorces* are rooted in the conditional Mosaic covenant. God uses different metaphors and analogies to show disfavor towards His people. None of these can rightly be stretched to say a man can divorce and remarry. Although God temporarily put Israel away, forgiveness of His people is always on the horizon. God is always seen as the permanent husband of Israel, even during times of punishment. At no time is it ever hinted that God completely forsook His people and married another wife. Hosea does not teach that Christians have the right to divorce and remarry. Rather, it teaches that God is gracious and forgiving to an adulterous people. The Christian should also be gracious and forgiving to an adulterous spouse.

Malachi 2

Ezra returned to Jerusalem in 458 BC. Nehemiah returned in 444 BC. They both encountered spiritual apathy and low moral standards by the Jews living in Jerusalem. Malachi prophesied between 450–430 BC. The people had external formal worship and were religious in offering sacrifices. Internally their hearts were not right before the Lord. This was shown in their daily lives. The people were living in sinful rebellion against God's Law. They were bringing lame, blind, and stolen animals for sacrifice (Mal. 1:6–14). Even the priests and Levites were corrupting justice (Mal. 2:1–9). The people were guilty of sorcery, perjury, and adultery. They were oppressing the poor, widows, aliens, and orphans (Mal. 3:5). They were robbing God of tithes and offerings (Mal. 3:8–12).

On top of all these sins they were profaning the Lord's holy institution of marriage. They were weeping and crying out to God to accept their sacrifices and offerings. God was not regarding them because of their corrupt and sinful lifestyles.

> Have we not all one father? Hath not one God created us? Why do we deal treacherously every man against his brother, by profaning the covenant of our fathers? Judah hath dealt treacherously; and an abomination is committed in Israel and in Jerusalem; for Judah hath profaned the holiness of the Lord which he loved, and hath married the daughter of a strange god. The Lord will cut off the man that doeth this, the master and the scholar, out of the tabernacles of Jacob, and him that offereth an offering unto the

Lord of hosts. And this have ye done again covering the altar of the Lord with tears, with weeping and with crying out, in so much that he regardeth not the offering any more, or receiveth it with good will at your hand. Yet ye say, wherefore? Because the Lord hath been witness between thee and the wife of thy youth, against whom thou hast dealt treacherously: yet she is thy companion, and the wife of thy covenant. And did not He make one? Yet had he the residue of the spirit. And wherefore one? That He might seek a godly seed. Therefore take heed to your spirit, and let none deal treacherously against the wife of his youth. For the Lord, the God of Israel, saith that He hateth putting away: for one covereth violence with his garment, saith the Lord of hosts: therefore take heed to your spirit, that ye deal not treacherously. Ye have wearied the Lord with your words. Yet ye say, Wherein have we wearied Him? When ye say, everyone that doeth evil is good in the sight of the Lord, and He delights in them; or, Where is the God of judgment? (Mal. 2:10–17)

Malachi begins verse 10 by arguing that since God created the Israelites, and He is their Father, they should not deal treacherously by profaning the covenant. He warns them that the man who marries *the daughter of a strange god* (an idolatrous woman) will be cut off. In verses 10–12 the Jews were said to be profaning the covenant given by God. God had specifically commanded Israel not to intermarry with pagan idolatrous people. God knew these marriages would lead Israel to follow other gods (Exod. 34:14–16; Deut. 7:1–4). Ezra and Nehemiah both dealt with this sin (Ezra 10; Neh. 13).

In verses 13–15 Malachi rebukes the people for not only marrying pagan women, but for divorcing their wives in order to do so. The sin of divorce is specifically mentioned as the reason God had no regard for their offerings. Verse 14 says the marriage of one's youth is a covenant. It calls the divorcing of one's wife *treachery*. Verse 15 also calls divorce *treachery*. Although this verse is difficult to translate, the context speaks of marriage and divorce. God made man and woman for the purpose of bearing godly offspring. Divorce is not conducive to nurturing godly children. The purposes of God were being corrupted by divorce and intermarriage with pagan wives. God warned the Jews not to deal treacherously with the wife of one's youth.

Verse 16 gives God's thoughts concerning divorce: *He hates it.* This is because it covers ones garment with violence. The phrase may be seen as "covering one's garment with sin," or "sin covering one's garment." The meaning is the same either way: wickedness will adhere to such a man and cannot be removed.

Malachi 2 concludes with the people questioning God. The context leads one to believe that the Jews saw no problem with divorcing their wives and remarrying. It is possible that they were divorcing and remarrying, and then claiming God's blessing upon such practices. God had already spoken on how He views these acts.

Conclusion

From Genesis to Malachi marriage is viewed as an important aspect of true religion. It has its foundation in the *one flesh* covenant (Gen. 1:27, 2:23–24). The unconditional Abrahamic covenant shows God's permanent relationship with the nation of Israel (Gen. 12:3). Marriage is used as a picture of God's faithfulness to Israel (Prov. 2:17; Isa. 54:1–10; Jer. 3:8; Hos. 3:1; Mal. 2:14). By the time of Moses, men were divorcing and remarrying for various reasons. The only legislation given by God was that a divorced and remarried woman could never return to her first husband. The woman was defiled. Returning to her original husband was an abomination to God. This would bring sin upon the land (Deut. 24:1–4). God did not approve of, nor establish, divorce. He claims He hates it and likens it to treachery (Mal. 2:15–16). Why did not God prohibit divorce and remarriage in the Mosaic Law? We are not told! He did not forbid polygamy or concubinage either. We do know that the Mosaic Law was temporal and given to regulate the hardness of man's heart. The Lord Jesus Christ came in the fullness of time and taught *all* God's righteous standards.

Chapter 2

The Gospels

Matthew 5

> It hath been said, whosoever shall put away his wife, let him give
> her a writing of divorcement: But I say unto you, that whosoever
> shall put away his wife, save for the cause of fornication, causeth
> her to commit adultery: and whosoever shall marry her that is di-
> vorced committeth adultery. (Matt. 5:31–32)

IVORCE AND remarkage are mentioned in six New Testament texts.
The first occurrence appears in "The Sermon on the Mount." This
sermon represents Jesus' relationship to the Law of God. Jesus was not presenting a rival system to the Law of Moses. His message was *fulfillment* of
the Law and the Prophets in contrast with the traditions of the Pharisees.
Christ taught the people that unless their righteousness surpassed that
of the scribes and the Pharisees, they could never enter the Kingdom of
Heaven (Matt. 5:20). This did not mean they could earn salvation by
obeying a higher standard of rules and regulations. Salvation came only
by faith in the Messiah. One point of this sermon was to show God's true
righteous standards as compared with the man-made traditions which had
been established by the Jews.

The religious leaders claimed a man could divorce his wife by simply
giving her a certificate of divorce. Those who were divorced were then free to
remarry. If this second marriage did not work, the process could be repeated
as often as necessary (cf. John 4:18). The theological school of Shammai
interpreted Deuteronomy 24:1–4 to mean that a man could only divorce
his wife and remarry for serious sexual sins. The school of Hillel interpreted
Deuteronomy 24:1–4 to mean that a man could divorce and remarry for
minor offenses. This is what "had been said" (Matt. 5:32).

The Lord Jesus Christ begins this section with stating the seventh
commandment, "you shall not commit adultery" (Matt. 5:27). Jesus gives

two examples of violations which His audience might not contemplate as adulterous; lust and remarriage. Whoever looks at a woman lustfully, commits adultery in his heart (Matt. 5:28). Whoever divorces and remarries, commits adultery (Matt. 5:32). The people had been told that if a man wanted a divorce, all he had to do was give his wife a certificate that would allow or even force her to depart. Both parties were then free to remarry. The certificate was a written bill of divorcement which was worded in this manner:

> On the _____ day of the week, the day of the month _____ , in the year _____ from the creation of the world, in the city of _____.
> I, _____ , the son of _____ , do willingly consent, being under no constraint, to release, to set free, and to put aside thee, my wife, _____ , daughter of _____ , who has been my wife before. Thus I do set free, release thee, and put thee aside, in order that thou may have permission and authority over thyself and to go and marry any man thou desire. No person may hinder thee from this day onward, and thou art permitted to every man. This shall be for thee from me a bill of dismissal, a letter of release, and a document of freedom, in accordance with the Law of Moses and Israel. _____ , the son of _____ , witness. _____ the son of _____ , witness.

Some claim that Matthew 5:32 agrees with this practice and furthermore allows Christians to divorce and remarry if their spouse commits adultery. They believe that adultery severs the one flesh bond and therefore Jesus must have used the word *porneia* (fornication) as an equivalent term for *moicheia* (adultery). English translations render this word in various ways: Fornication (KJV); Sexual Immorality (NKJV); Unchastity—Matthew 5:32 and Immorality—Matthew 19:9 (NASB); Marital Unfaithfulness (NIV); Unchastity (RSV). The NIV comes closest to rendering this word as adultery yet falls short. The NIV uses the dynamic equivalent (thought for thought) theory rather than a more literal (word for word) rendering of the biblical text. The translators of the NIV may have substituted their interpretation into the text rather than letting the reader decide the issue for their self.

The Bible student must determine what *porneia* and *moicheia* mean in context. Strong's Concordance codes each Greek word to a number. This allows those who are unfamiliar with the Greek language to look up the basic definition of any given word. This can then be cross referenced with other biblical passages. *Porneia* and its cognates are coded as follows: *porneia*/4202; *porneuo*/4203; *porne*/4204; *pornos*/4205. *Moicheia* and its cognates are coded as follows: *moicheia*/3430; *moichalis*/3428; *moichao*/3429; *moicheuo*/3431; *moichos*/3432.

Lexical Study

Five Greek Lexicons will be examined to find the definition or range of meaning for the terms *porneia* and *moicheia*. The criteria for choosing these lexicons is as follows: A. Length of time in print. Have they been published for a sufficient length of time so as to allow grammarians the chance to correct any errors? B. Acceptance by students and scholars. Are they widely used by Greek teachers and students from various backgrounds because of their precision and accuracy? C. Historical Research. Have the authors and editors researched a broad enough source of Greek literature to enable them to give an accurate range of meaning to each word? The Lexical definitions given for *porneia*, *moicheia*, and their cognates are as follows:

G. Abbott-Smith, *A Manual Greek Lexicon of the New Testament*, published by T. & T. Clark (1921). Last reprint 1968.

porneia	Fornication is the basic definition. Distinguished from adultery. May equal adultery because Sirach 23:23 uses it this way. Used metaphorically of idolatry.
porneuo	To prostitute the body for hire. To commit fornication. Idolatry.
porne	A prostitute or harlot. Metaphorically for Babylon (i.e. Rome).
pornos	A male prostitute. A fornicator.
moicheia	Adultery.
moichalis	An adulteress.
moichao	To commit adultery with.
moicheuo	To commit adultery.
moichos	An adulterer.

G. Kittel and G. Friedrich, translated by Geoffrey W. Bromiley, *Theological Dictionary of the New Testament*, published by W. Kohlhammer Verlag (1933). Last reprint 1992.

Non-Jewish usage

porneia	Fornication or licentiousness.
porneia	Fornication
porneuo	To prostitute or commit fornication.
porne	A harlot for hire (usually referred to slaves).
pornos	A whoremonger or male prostitute.

The Old Testament (Septuagint)

porneia	Fornication sometimes involving adultery.
porneuo	To play the harlot (sometimes involving adultery). It may be used of the prostitute or a betrothed woman who proves to be unfaithful.
porne	Harlot.
pornos	Does not appear in the Old Testament. Only appears in the Apocrypha during this time.

The New Testament

porneia	The problem in Matthew 5:32 and 19:9 is perhaps that Jewish Christians who keep the Law are required to divorce adulterous wives and hence cannot be responsible if these contract a new relationship which is from a Christian stand-point itself adulterous. Divorce itself is not conceded. In John 8:41 the Jews claimed they were not born of fornication (*porneia*). Acts 15:20, 29; 21:15 requires the Gentile Christians to avoid fornication (cf. Leviticus 17–18). Porneia has no part in God's kingdom.
porneuo	Degeneracy.
porne	Degeneracy. The center of paganism with its harlot-like apostasy from God.
pornos	Excluded in I Corinthians 6:9 and Ephesians 5:5.
moicheia	Adultery.
moichalis	Adulteress or adulterous.
moichao	To commit adultery with.

moicheuo	To commit adultery.
moichos	Adulterer.

The Apostolic Fathers

porneia	Hermas *Mandates* 4.1.1 warns against *porneia*, which differs from, but also includes, adultery (cf. *Mandates* 8.3; 4.1.5). We do not find the transferred use in the apostolic fathers, who abandon the terminology of the O.T. prophets.

J. Moulton and G. Milligan, *The Vocabulary of the Greek New Testament*, published by WM. B. Eerdmans (1930). Last printed 1976.

porneia	Originally meant prostitution or fornication. Came to be applied to unlawful sexual intercourse. It was a wider term than adultery, embracing the idea of barter or sexual vice. In the Old Testament there was a tendency to assimilate the two terms.
porneuo	To commit fornication.
porne	Prostitute.
pornos	A male prostitute, but generally understood in the N.T. in the sense of fornication.
moicheia	Adultery.
moichalis	A married woman who commits adultery.
moichao	To commit adultery with.
moicheuo	To commit adultery.
moichos	Adulterer.

H. G. Liddell and R. Scott, *A Greek-English Lexicon*, published by Oxford University Press (1843). Last printed 1996.

porneia	Prostitution. Refers to fornication in Matthew 19:9. Metaphorically of idolatry.
porneuo	To become a prostitute.
porne	A harlot or prostitute.
pornos	A catamite, sodomite, or fornicator.
moicheia	Adultery.
moichalis	Adulteress.
moichao	To commit adultery.
moicheuo	To commit adultery.
moichos	Adulterer, sodomite, or idolatrous person.

W. Bauer and W. Arndt and F. W. Gingrich, *A Greek-English Lexicon Of The New Testament and Other Early Christian Literature*, Published by University of Chicago Press (1952). Last printed 1974.

porneia	Basic definition is fornication, prostitution, or unchastity. Of every kind of unlawful sexual intercourse. Differentiated from adultery in Matthew 15:19 and Mark 7:21. Appears as adultery in Sirach 23:23. Sexual unfaithfulness of the married woman in Matthew 5:32; 19:9. An illegitimate or bastard child. In the Old Testament as a symbol of apostasy from God or idolatry.
porneuo	To prostitute or practice sexual immorality. Distinguished from committing adultery.
porne	A prostitute or harlot.
pornos	A fornicator, one who practices immorality. Differentiated from an adulterer.
moicheia	Adultery.
moichalis	Adulteress.
moichao	To commit adultery.
moicheuo	To commit adultery.
moichos	Adulterer.

When performing lexical research it is important to consult quality scholarship sources. One example of poor quality scholarship is found in *Vine's Complete Expository Dictionary*. Under the heading *Fornication* Vine writes:

> In Matt. 5:32 and 19:9 it stands for, or includes adultery; it is distinguished from it in 15:19 and Mark 7:21.

Although it is true that the term fornication can include adultery in limited contexts, this is in not definite in the context of Matt. 5:32 and 19:9. It is improbable that it "stands for" adultery as Vine asserts. He correctly understands that in Matt. 15:19 and Mark 7:21 that two words *porneia* and *moicheia* are used in the same context to distinguish between the two. He fails to realize that this is most likely done in Matt. 5:32 and 19:9 for the same reason. In determining the meaning of words in their intended context it is not enough to state what is possible based upon a broad range of lexical definitions. The job of the expositor is to determine the most probable usage of the word in context.

New Testament Survey

A study of relevant New Testament passages may shed light on how the term *porneia* could be interpreted. We will examine New Testament texts other than Matthew 5:32 and 19:9 where the term *porneia* is used. Special attention will be paid to passages where *porneia* and *moicheia* are used in the same context.

> Matthew 15:19. *Porneia* and *moicheia* are used in the same sentence to differentiate between the two sins.
>
> Mark 7:21. *Porneia* and *moicheia* are used in the same sentence to differentiate between the two sins.
>
> John 8:41. The Pharisees accused Jesus of being born of *porneia*. In this context *porneia* refers to unlawful sexual relations during the betrothal period.
>
> Acts 15:20, 29 and 21:25. *Porneia* is one of four things which Gentiles are to abstain from. In this context *porneia* refers to the unlawful incestuous marriages listed in Leviticus 18:6–18.
>
> Romans 1:29. *Porneia* refers to sexual deviancy in general.
>
> First Corinthians 5:1. The incestuous man who has his father's wife is committing *porneia*.
>
> First Corinthians 6:13, 18. *Porneia* refers to sexual deviancy in general. No claim is made whether the man who joins himself to the harlot is married or not.
>
> First Corinthians 7:2. *Porneia* is used as a term for sexual deviancy in general.
>
> Second Corinthians 12:21. *Porneia* is used as a term for sexual deviancy in general.
>
> Galatians 5:19. *Porneia* and *moicheia* are used in the same sentence to differentiate between the two sins.
>
> Ephesians 5:3, 5. *Porneia* refers to sexual deviancy in general.
>
> Colossians 3:5. *Porneia* refers to sexual deviancy in general.

First Thessalonians 4:3. *Porneia* refers to sexual deviancy in general.

Revelation 2:21. *Porneia* refers to sexual deviancy in general.

Revelation 9:21. *Porneia* refers to sexual deviancy in general.

Revelation 14:8; 17:2, 4; 18:3; and 19:2. *Porneia* is used to refer to spiritual harlotry or apostasy.

Cognates that are related to the word *porneia* appear 29 times in other New Testament passages. The words *porneia* and *moicheia* are clearly differentiated in the following passages.

First Corinthians 6:9. *Pornoi* and *mochoi* are used in the same sentence to differentiate between the two sins.

Hebrews 13:4. *Pornos* and *moichous* are used in the same sentence to differentiate between the two sins.

Those who wish to study the remaining 27 passages will find the following definitions are used: 1) Sexual deviancy in general. 2) A prostitute. 3) Spiritual harlotry or apostasy.

Summary

Porneia means fornication or prostitution. It is often used for sexual deviancy in general. This may include homosexuality, incest, polygamy, adultery, pre-marital sexual relations, or prostitution. In certain contexts the New Testament does limit the meaning of *porneia* to specify spiritual apostasy, incestuous marriages, or unlawful sexual relations committed during the betrothal period. There is no evidence that *porneia* is used as an exact one-to-one, no more no less, equivalent for adultery in the entire New Testament.

Moicheia means adultery. Some Lexicons claim Sirach 23:23 uses *porneia* as a synonym for adultery. This usage in Sirach is far from certain. Sirach is an Apocryphal book of wisdom literature written about 200 BC. The phrase used is "in fornication she committed adultery" (*en porneia emoicheusthe*). Joseph Jensen, possibly the author of the finest article examining the uses of *porneia* in relevant literature, translates Sirach 23:23

"she wantonly committed adultery."[1] Bruce Vawter believes it is difficult to prove Sirach 23:23 uses *porneia* as an equivalent to marital infidelity.[2] Abel Isaksson thinks that *porneia* in Sirach 23:23 refers to the 'sexual desire' that led the woman to commit adultery.[3] The same is probably true of *porneia* as recorded in The Shepherd of Hermas Mandate 4.1.5 and Tobit 8:7. If Sirach did use *porneia* as an expression for adultery this in no way proves that Jesus or any other biblical writers used the word in this manner. New Testament authors use the terms *porneia* and *moicheia* together when they wish to differentiate between the two sins. Most commentators do not hesitate to admit that Matthew 15:19 and Mark 7:21 use *moicheia* and *porneia* in the same sentence to differentiate between the two. It is most probable that Matthew 5:32 and 19:9 intend to show a distinction also.

Interpretative Study

Some claim that Matthew 5:31–32 teaches a man may divorce his adulterous wife and then remarry. In verse 31 Jesus is merely recounting what Rabbinic tradition allowed. He does not give approval of this practice. He told His listeners to be "perfect, as your Father in heaven is perfect" (Matt. 5:48). Every other point of the "Sermon on the Mount" reflects a higher standard than the Rabbinic traditions of Jesus' day. Why would this subject be the one exception? Those who claim a person can divorce and remarry in cases of adultery are simply making Jesus a disciple of Shammai. Jesus would not be upholding the ideal but would be teaching an ideal with one exception.

Edersheim writes:

> It is a serious mistake on the part of commentators to set the teaching of Christ on this subject by the side of that of Shammai.[4]

Will Durant writes:

> He [Jesus] hardened the Law in matters of sex and divorce.[5]

Although Durant is not entirely correct in his statement he rightly understands that Jesus taught a higher standard than the scribes and Pharisees. It is not so much that Jesus hardened the Law but that Jesus

1. Joseph Jensen, "Does *Porneia* mean Fornication," p. 172–173.
2. Bruce Vawter, "Divorce and the New Testament," p. 531.
3. Abel Isaksson, "Marriage and Ministry in the New Temple," p. 133–34.
4. Alfred Edersheim, *Life and Times of Jesus the Messiah*, p. 245.
5. Will Durant, *Caesar and Christ*, p. 568.

taught God's true righteous standard. If lust is seen as breaking the seventh commandment (Matt. 5:27–30) it should not surprise us to find divorce and remarriage condemned in similar terms (Matt. 5:32). Jesus claimed that adultery could be mental as well as physical.

Matthew 5:32 is phrased in this manner:

> But I say to you that whoever divorces his wife except for a matter of *porneia*/fornication, makes her *moichasthai*/commit adultery; and whoever marries a woman who is divorced *moichatai*/commits adultery.

When interpreting this passage attention must be paid to the fact that the "exception clause" appears only in Matthew's *Jewish* Gospel. The cultural and historical context must be taken into consideration. The man in Jewish society was not simply allowed to divorce a fornicating wife, he was compelled. If his wife was found to have committed sexual sin, he would have no choice but to put her away. This is true both during the betrothal period as well as after a consummated marriage. According to Rabbinic Law, the wife could intentionally cause the man to divorce her by being unfaithful. The man would have no say in the matter. Both Roman and Jewish cultures compelled a man to divorce an unfaithful wife; both during betrothal and after consummation. Both Roman and Jewish cultures compelled the remarriage of a divorced woman. When she remarried, Christ claimed that she would commit adultery. Matthew 5:32 teaches that the man, who divorced his wife for any other reason except fornication, was the cause of her adultery. This does not mean a wife who was put away for adultery was allowed to remarry. Rather, it teaches that when *porneia* has been committed by the woman, her husband is not the *cause* of her adultery, she is. If the wife was unfaithful, it was she and not the man who was responsible for the divorce and the subsequent adulterous remarriage.

In this case the exception merely exempts Jesus' disciples from the *responsibility* for the divorce which an unfaithful wife brings about. These teachings relieve the man of the responsibility for the divorce and its consequences. The wife bears the responsibility. Remarriage is still called adulterous. This is what the "exception clause" means.

Augustine in his exposition of *Our Lord's Sermon on the Mount* has this to say about the exception clause listed in Matthew's gospel:

> Wherefore did he not add, saving for the cause of fornication, which the Lord permits, unless because he wishes a similar rule to be understood, that if he shall put away his wife (which he

is permitted to do for the cause of fornication), he is to remain without a wife, or be reconciled to his wife? . . . And for this reason also, because He who says, It is not lawful to put away one's wife saving for the cause of fornication, forces him to retain his wife, if there should be no cause of fornication: but if there should be, He does not force him to put her away, but permits him, just as when it is said, let it not be lawful for a woman to marry another, unless her husband be dead; if she shall marry before the death of her husband, she is guilty; if she shall not marry after the death of her husband, she is not guilty, for she is not commanded to marry, but merely permitted . . . Now when He says, "saving for the cause of fornication," He has not said of which of them, whether the man or the woman. For not only is it allowed to put away a wife who commits fornication; but whoever puts away that wife even by whom he is himself compelled to commit fornication, puts her away undoubtedly for the cause of fornication. . . . But in reference to what He says, "whosoever shall marry her that is divorced commits adultery," it may be asked whether she also who is married commits adultery in the same way as he does who marries her. For she is also commanded to remain unmarried, or be reconciled to her husband; but this in the case of her departing from her husband. There is however, a great difference whether she put away or is put away. For if she put away her husband, and marries another, she seems to have left her former husband from a desire of changing her marriage connection, which is, without doubt, an adulterous thought. But if she is put away by the husband, with whom she desired to be, he indeed who marries her commits adultery, according to the Lord's declaration; but whether she also be involved in a like crime is uncertain—although it is much less easy to discover how, when a man and woman have intercourse one with another with equal consent, one of them should be an adulterer, and the other not. To this is to be added the consideration, that if he commits adultery by marrying her who is divorced from her husband (although she does not put away, but is put away), she causes him to commit adultery, which nevertheless the Lord forbids. And hence we infer that, whether she has been put away, or has put away her husband, it is necessary for her to remain unmarried or be reconciled to her husband.

Some modern writers wrongly teach that Jesus gave an exception for remarriage after divorce in Matthew 5:32 without calling it adultery. Their logic is manifestly absurd. It would make no sense at all for Jesus to claim the woman who was divorced for *porneia* was allowed to remarry while the woman who was divorced for any other reason was not. Jesus clearly refutes this kind of thinking by stating "whoever marries a divorced woman commits adultery," He gives no exceptions.

Summary

Matthew 5:32 places the emphasis of the guilt on the husband who divorces for unwarranted reasons. The exception clause is given to show that in the one exception, *fornication*, the primary blame lies not with the man, but with the woman. The remarriage is still adultery but the blame is shifted from the man to the woman. The exception clause is simply a matter of fact recognition that the woman has already committed fornication. She is responsible for the divorce, he is not. This does not allow her to remarry. The last part of verse 32 makes it clear by claiming "whoever shall marry her that is divorced commits adultery." Jesus taught a higher moral standard than either Hillel or Shammai. Every standard given in Matthew 5–7 surpasses the righteousness of the scribes and the Pharisees. This subject is no *exception*.

Matthew 19

The Pharisees also came unto him, tempting him, and saying unto him, Is it lawful for a man to put away his wife for every cause? And he answered and said unto them, Have you not read, that he which made them at the beginning made them male and female, and said, For this cause shall a man leave father and mother, and shall cleave to his wife: and they twain shall become one flesh? Wherefore they are no longer twain, but one flesh. What therefore God hath joined together, let no man put asunder. They said unto him, Why did Moses then command to give a writing of divorcement, and put her away? He saith unto them, Moses because of the hardness of your hearts suffered you to put away your wives: but from the beginning it was not so. And I say unto you, Whosoever shall put away his wife, except it be for fornication, and shall marry another, committeth adultery: and whoso marrieth her which is put away doth commit adultery. His disciples say unto him, If the case of the man be so with his wife, it is not good to marry. But he said unto them, all men cannot receive this saying, save they to whom it is given. For there are some eunuchs, which were so born from their mother's womb: and there are some eunuchs, which were made eunuchs of men: and there be eunuchs, which have made themselves eunuchs for the kingdom of heaven's sake. He that is able to receive it, let him receive it. (Matthew 19:3–12)

Differing views. Six interpretations of the 'exception clause' are listed below:

God Forgives

This view states that since God forgives, the divorcee may remarry. God may consider remarriage adultery but if remarriage meets a person's *needs*, then it is allowed; God will forgive them. It is believed that God wants people to be happy or fulfilled. If a person *needs* their sexual, emotional, or financial desires fulfilled then this overrides the fact that God calls remarriage after divorce sin. This interpretation is built on half-truths and very little exegesis. It is true that God forgives sin. It is not true that forgiveness allows the believer to break His commands. It is true that God wants fulfilled children. Fulfillment comes only from obeying Christ. This view is really no more than an excuse for sin without the need for repentance.

It is interesting to note that many who hold this view normally expect God to forgive them if they divorce their spouse and remarry but they themselves have no intention of forgiving their spouse of any wrongs they may have committed. This is called hardness of heart. Jesus warned against this in the parable of the unjust slave (Matt. 18:23–35). Those who have been forgiven by God should be willing to forgive others. The husband or wife who expects to be forgiven by God should be willing to forgive their spouse.

Erasmian Adultery

This view is called Erasmian because the basic conclusion was given its greatest impetus by Erasmus in the 16th century. To be precise there is an old Erasmian interpretive method and a new Erasmian interpretive method. Both are termed Erasmian because of the common conclusion that the innocent spouse may divorce and remarry in cases of adultery or desertion.

Erasmus and many of the Reformers held to this conclusion because of a form of interpretive legal fiction that saw the adulterous spouse as figuratively dead. Modern Erasmians hinge their conclusions on the following three major assumptions: First, Jesus was speaking of the same kind of divorce as the Jews were. Namely, adultery dissolves the one flesh bond which gives a person the right to divorce and remarry. Second, the *exception clause* modifies both the preceding verb phrase "whoever divorces his wife" as well as the following verb phrase "and marries another." Third, *porneia* is a one to one equivalent for adultery. All three of these assumptions are implausible.

Problems with the old Erasmian Interpretation include:

The interpretive legal fiction method, as originally held by Erasmus and some of the Reformers, has been shown to be faulty. Because of this it has basically been abandoned by those who support divorce and remarriage. Since the old Erasmian method of allowing divorce and remarriage was proved deficient new interpretive methods are now used to achieve the same results.

Problems with the new Erasmian method include:

First, although it is true that both Jewish and Roman divorce laws allowed both parties the freedom to remarry in cases of adultery, this does not mean that Jesus agreed with this practice. Jesus often clashed with the traditions of men. We may have here in the Matthean Gospel texts clear examples of the difference between the law of God and the laws of men. This would certainly answer the question as to why the disciples reacted so strongly to the teaching of the Lord: "If such is the case of the man with his wife, it is better not to marry" (Matt. 19:10). If Jesus were teaching that a man could divorce his adulterous wife and remarry one would not expect such a surprised reaction from the disciples. Jesus would basically be teaching the same thing as the house of Shammai.

The incorrect application of this cultural understanding of divorce laws has led to further error. Since Jewish and Romans laws allowed remarriage after divorce for any reason it is taught that Jesus must have allowed remarriage after divorce for any reason also. This clearly contradicts the teaching of the New Testament.

Second, there is no biblical evidence to support the Erasmian claim that adultery ends or dissolves the one flesh marriage bond. Many Erasmian interpreters are reluctant to claim that one act of adultery dissolves the one flesh bond and allows divorce and remarriage. For this reason the normative claim is that it is *persistent* adultery that ends the marriage and allows one to divorce and remarry. The term "persistent" is vague and undefined. Are three acts of adultery considered *persistent*; ten, twenty, one hundred? Who is to decide how many acts of adultery are considered persistent? To what degree must adultery persist until divorce is allowed? Jesus told His disciples to forgive seventy times seven which is a way of saying that Christians should forgive as many times as necessary (Matt. 18:22). The Christian is to forgive their unfaithful spouse and pray for reconciliation. They are not divorce them and find another spouse. No matter how persistent the sin, reconciliation is always an option until either spouse dies.

Another problem with the *persistent* adultery theory is we are not told *when* the persistent adultery is discovered. The normative Erasmian assumption is that the adultery of the guilty spouse is discovered early on by the innocent spouse. After this the guilty spouse continues to commit adultery for an extended period of time. It is this continuous adultery, after being discovered, that we are told, allows the innocent spouse to divorce the guilty one.

What if the adultery persists for years before the innocent spouse discovers it? What if, as soon as the guilty spouse is discovered, the guilty spouse repents and ceases their sin? Erasmians who are consistent would need to claim that the one flesh bond was dissolved because the adultery was *persistent*. What if the guilty spouse had adulterous affairs for years, then ceased, and the innocent spouse did not learn of the unfaithfulness for years after the fact? The Erasmian position would lead one to believe that the innocent spouse could divorce the guilty one even if the adultery had ceased years before. This is because Erasmians teach that Jesus allowed divorce and remarriage in cases of *persistent* adultery.

A related problem with the Erasmian interpretation is their claim that the "innocent" spouse in matters of adultery has the right to remarry. By default this means that the "guilty" spouse does not. If the marriage bond is truly ended by adultery or divorce then it makes no sense for only the innocent party to have the right remarry. If the marriage is irreconcilably ended then both parties would have the right to remarry. The teaching that the innocent party is free to remarry is based upon the erroneous belief that adultery breaks the marriage bond. If this was true and the innocent party forgave the guilty party, they would need to be remarried.

Second, it is doubtful that *porneia* is a one to one equivalent for adultery. Every other time in the New Testament where the words *porneia* and *moicheia* are used together it is done for the purpose of distinguishing between the two. It is most probable that Jesus used the word *porneia* to refer to something other than adultery. There are at least three other reasonable explanations of the meaning of "except fornication" in Matthew 19:9. If any of them are true then the Erasmian interpretation falls.

Third, it is probable that the *exception clause* modifies only the preceding "whoever divorces his wife" and not the following "and marries another" phrase. Neither Erasmus, a Greek scholar, nor the Reformers make any reference to the exception clause modifying both the preceding and the following verb phrases. They resorted to the use of Old Testament legal fiction.

The Erasmian view is based upon the belief that "two wrongs make a right." If one spouse wrongs the other by committing adultery (has sexual relations outside the marriage bond) then the other spouse can also break their vows and have sexual relations outside of the original marriage bond. One emphasis of the teachings of Jesus is forgiveness. The followers of Jesus Christ are to forgive even their enemies and pray for those who mistreat them (Matt. 5:44; Luke 6:28). To Erasmians these commands of Christ to forgive do not seem to apply to spouses. If a spouse sins against them by committing adultery they can divorce that spouse and find another one. If taken to its logical conclusion the Erasmian position would allow a person to divorce and remarry every time their *current* spouse commits a sin qualified under the "exception clause." Under this scenario one could theoretically be divorced and remarried dozens of times, all with the approval and blessing of the Lord.

Unlawful Marriage to Gentile Idolaters

In Ezra's day the Jews were required to divorce their Gentile wives in order to keep the Jewish ancestral lineage free from impurity and idolatry (Ezra 9–10; Neh. 13). Some have applied this to mean that a Christian may divorce an unbelieving spouse and remarry. There are at least three problems with this view. First, most marriages take place between two Gentiles. It would make no sense for God to command Gentiles to divorce in order to keep their lineage pure. Second, First Corinthians 7:12–13 makes it clear that a believing spouse is not to divorce their unbelieving partner as long as they consent to live with them. Third, what took place in the restoration community under the leadership of Ezra and Nehemiah was a unique occurrence. The separation from Gentile wives was necessary to insure the continued existence of the Jewish nation (Deut. 7:3–4).

Incestuous Marriages

This view is sometimes called the Rabbinic view. It teaches that fornication refers to unlawful marriages which are prohibited in Leviticus 18:6–18. Some leading adherents of this view include W. K. Lowther Clarke, F. F. Bruce, J. Carl Laney, J. A. Fitzmeyer, and Charles C. Ryrie.

Leviticus 18:6–18 deals with prohibitions of incestuous marriages. The phrase used is "you shall not uncover the nakedness of." This is a Hebrew euphemism for sexual intercourse in the confines of an incestuous marriage. A man was not allowed to marry his mother, sister, daughter, granddaughter, niece, aunt, mother-in-law, daughter-in-law, or sister-in-law. Incestuous marriage may be what Christ meant when He said "whoever divorces his wife except for fornication." First Corinthians 5:1 may refer to a man marrying his father's widow. This would be a flagrant violation of Leviticus 18:8.

Acts 15 uses the term *porneia* to refer to incestuous marriages. Some converts from the Pharisees had come down from Judea and were teaching the Gentile believers that unless they were circumcised and kept the law of Moses they could not be saved (Acts 15:1). Paul, Barnabas, and other brethren met at Jerusalem to discuss this issue. After much debate they were led by the Holy Spirit to tell the Gentile converts that they should abstain from idols, things that were strangled, blood, and fornication (Acts 15:20, 29). These are the things which are listed in Leviticus 17:10—18:18. It seems to be assumed that a believer would abstain from adultery, bestiality, homosexuality, and sacrificing of children (Lev. 18:20–23).

The Jerusalem Council would have no need to tell believers to refrain from fornication if it meant adultery or other sexual perversions in this context. The evidence points to them telling the Gentile believers not to enter into incestuous marriages. These four prohibitions may have been designed to promote peace between Jewish and Gentile believers. Gentiles were not to practice those things which were offensive to Jewish brethren. Some believe these four prohibitions are binding on Christians for all time. In either case, this would explain why Matthew would include this exception clause in his Gospel to Jewish readers.

Some may wonder how probable it is that a person would enter into an incestuous marriage? The Romans had laws against incest but they were not as strict as the Mosaic Law. They also did not seem to be well enforced. The Bible gives us the narrative of Herod Antipas. Herodias was the wife of Herod Philip I. Herodias was the niece of Herod Philip I, which means she was married to her uncle. Herodias was also the niece of Herod Antipas. Herod Antipas and Herod Philip I were half brothers. Herod Philip I and Herodias divorced. Herodias remarried Herod Antipas. Now Herod Antipas was married to his half-brother's wife who was also his niece. According to Leviticus 18:11 and 20:21, these were illegal incestuous marriages. Not because she was considered his brother's wife but because she was his niece. Some believe that John the Baptist was thrown into prison and beheaded for preaching against this sin. The weakness of this assumption is the biblical text states that John told Herod "It is not lawful for you to have your brother's wife" (Mark 6:18). John did not say it is not lawful for you to marry your niece. It appears that the emphasis of John's preaching was against the sin of divorce and remarriage itself.

Josephus also reports the practice of incest among Roman rulers. Archelaus divorced his wife and married Glaphyra, the former wife of his half-brother. Bernice was originally married to her uncle, Herod Chalcis. Bernice also had an incestuous relationship with her brother, Herod Agrippa II. Bazeus married his sister, Helena.

Betrothal

Unlike western societies which practice engagement, the Jewish culture practiced betrothal. Betrothal was a binding legal contract that could only be broken by death or divorce. The betrothed couple were considered husband and wife. The marriage was usually arranged by parents. The bride price or dowry was paid to the father of the bride for economic loss to the family. This would compensate the father for the daughter's work he would lose. He could earn interest off the dowry but it was not to be spent in case his daughter was widowed or divorced. Next, a betrothal promise was made, but the marriage was not yet consummated. During this time the bride would prepare herself for marriage. The groom would prepare a home for them, usually in his father's house. At the end of one year, a ceremony and wedding feast took place. During the feast, the bride and groom would go into the bridal chamber and consummate the marriage. A cloth would be brought out to prove the bride's virginity. If the bride was found to not be a virgin, either before the wedding or at the time of consummation, she was to be divorced. This is why weddings of virgins were usually held on Wednesdays and weddings of widows were held on Thursdays. The courts sat on Mondays and Thursdays. If it became evident to the groom on Wednesday night that his bride was not a virgin, he could go to court on Thursday and bring suit against her and her father.

This was the situation Joseph thought he was in with Mary. This also explains why the Jews claimed Jesus was born of fornication (John 8:41). Before the marriage was consummated Mary was found to be pregnant. Joseph was not simply allowed to divorce Mary; Jewish law compelled him to do so. Joseph was a righteous man so he sought to divorce her secretly. If Joseph sought to divorce Mary publicly this could have led to her death by stoning. It was not up to Joseph to stone his betrothed for the sin of fornication it was the men of the city who would do so (Deut. 22:20–21).

Luke 2:5 only mentions the betrothal to his Greek-Gentile readers. Matthew 1:18–25 gives a fuller account to his Jewish readers. The betrothal view teaches that *porneia* is premarital sexual relations between a betrothed person and a third outside party. It takes into account Matthew's inclusion of the 'exception clause' to his Jewish audience. Christ stated a consummated marriage was permanent until death. One could divorce his betrothed wife because of *porneia*. This view has been proposed by James Montgomery Boice, Abel Isaksson, and Lehman Strauss.

The strengths of the Betrothal view include:

1. Every other time in the New Testament that *porneia* (fornication) and *moicheia* (adultery) are used together it is done to differentiate between the two sins. It is probable that this is done in Matthew 19:9 also.

2. There is no evidence that Jesus used the word fornication to refer to broader sexual sins which included adultery.

3. The betrothal view takes into consideration the reason why the "exception clause" is listed in Matthew's Jewish Gospel and not the Gospels of Mark and Luke which were written primarily to Gentile readers.

4. There is an example of the righteous practice of this type of divorce listed earlier in Mathew's Gospel (Matt. 1:18–20).

5. This view explains the surprised reaction of the disciples in Matthew 19:10.

One interesting fact should be considered. As far as I know none of the early Christian writers mention the betrothal view. Almost all of them quote Matthew 5:32 when mentioning the "exception clause." Some quote from Matthew 19 but few, if any, quote Matthew 19:9 directly. It is often assumed that the "exception clause" in Mathew 5:32 refers to the same thing as Matthew 19:9. Could it be that Matthew 5:32 prohibits remarriage after divorce for consummated marriages while Matthew 19:9 refers to betrothals? This could be one explanation as to why the early Christian writers quoted from Matthew's Gospel but did not hold the betrothal view. For the modern Christian who is wondering how each view might apply to his life; both the betrothal view and the early Christian view prohibit remarriage after divorce for any reason.

The Early Church View

The early Church taught that *porneia* meant sexual deviancy in general, but it was not limited to adultery. If a man's wife committed *fornication*, he was to separate from her until she repented of her sin. He was then to receive her back with the same love with which Christ loved the Church. To live with an unrepentant adulterous wife was a sin; to not forgive her was also a sin. If a legal divorce took place, remarriage while one's spouse was alive was still prohibited. This view is so named because it was held by a virtual consensus of the early church for the first six hundred years.

The strengths of the Early Church view include:

1. It best explains the placement of the "exception clause" in the Lord's teaching on divorce and remarriage.

2. This view explains the surprised reaction of the disciples in Matthew 19:10.

3. It explains the inclusion of the "exception clause" in Matthew's Gospel since a Jew would have been compelled to divorce his wife who had committed fornication.

4. Fornication is not a one to one equivalent with adultery.

Interpretive Study

The Pharisees came to test Jesus. Three motives have been proposed as to why they asked this question. 1) They were attempting to get Jesus to incriminate Himself by speaking against the Mosaic Law (actually it would be against their interpretation of the Law since the Law did not specifically address the issue of divorce and remarriage). 2) They wanted to know what Jesus' interpretation of Deuteronomy 24:1–4 would be. Would Jesus side with the house of Hillel or the house of Shammai? 3) Since John the Baptist had recently been beheaded for speaking against the divorce and remarriage of Herod, they were attempting to get Jesus to say something against the political authorities.

Mishna, *Gittin* 9.10 reads:

> The school of Shammai says: A man may not divorce his wife unless he has found unchastity in her, for it is written, Because he has found in her indecency in anything. And the school of Hillel says: He may divorce her even if she spoiled a dish for him, for it is written, because he has found in her indecency in anything. Rabbi Akiba says: Even if she found another fairer than she, for it is written, and it shall be if she found no favor in his eyes.

Gittin is the plural form of the Hebrew word *get* (divorce). The laws of *gittin* only allow for divorce initiated by the husband. If there was just cause for a man to divorce his wife, the court *required* him to do so. If a husband refused the court's demand to divorce his wife he is subject to penalties including excommunication, monetary fines, or physical punishment. The above mentioned opinion of Rabbi Akiba (AD 50–135) may not have been a factor in Jesus' day since Akiba was not born until after Jesus was crucified.

It appears that this group of Pharisees held to the dominant view of Hillel. They did not ask if a divorced man could remarry. They assumed that any divorced person could remarry. They wanted to know if a man could divorce his wife for any reason. The answer they received surprised them! Instead of entering into a debate over the interpretation of Deuteronomy 24:1–4, Jesus by-passed their traditions and took them back to the beginning of creation, Genesis 1 and 2. To Jesus, man and wife were one flesh. Because God had joined them together, no man was to separate them (Matt. 19:6). The Jews retorted with the Mosaic concession. They claimed Moses *commanded* a man to divorce his wife. Jesus replied that Moses only allowed this to happen because of the hardness of man's heart. From the beginning of time this was not God's plan.

Up until verse 9, all agree that Jesus taught an absolute prohibition of divorce and remarriage. It is verse 9 that causes people problems. The main reason for this is that few Christians take into account the cultural and Jewish legal considerations when examining the 'exception clause' in Matthew's gospel. Matthew records one exception for divorce when writing to his Jewish readers. Mark writes to Romans and gives no exception for divorce. What does the "exception clause" mean? The Pharisees wanted to know under what circumstances a man was allowed to divorce his wife. Jesus answered their question, *porneia*. The societal structure under which the Jews lived did not merely allow a man to divorce his wife, it compelled him. A man in Jewish culture, who found his wife to be guilty of *porneia*, would be compelled by society to divorce her. This could mean a man's wife was found to be guilty of sexual sin after consummating a legal marriage. It may simply be speaking of the man who found his wife to have lost her virginity before their wedding night.

It is possible that Matthew 19:9 should be understood in a similar manner as Matthew 5:32. Since the culture of Jesus' time compelled a man to divorce a fornicating spouse, then Jesus does not hold his followers responsible for the divorce of a wife who has committed *porneia*. The Pharisees asked the question: "Is it lawful for a man to divorce his wife for any reason?" The answer was no! A man can not divorce his wife for any reason, except *porneia*. Lest they should think that the man had the right to remarry, Jesus added, "and marries another commits adultery." Some have assumed that since the Pharisees used the word divorce to include the right to remarry, then Jesus *must have* used the word in the same way. It is true that the Jews of Jesus' day believed the right to remarry came with the right to divorce. Is it correct to assume that Jesus must have taught the same kind of divorce that the Jews practiced? To assume this wrongly makes Judaism, not the teaching of Christ, the decisive factor in interpreting Scripture.

The burden of proof lies with those who claim that Jesus was using the term "divorce" in the same manner as the Pharisees; namely, divorce with the right to remarry. Lest they should think that the woman had the right to remarry, Jesus added, "and whoever marries her who is divorced commits adultery." Some translations (NIV, RSV, and NASB) that are founded on the eclectic Critical Greek Text omit this final phrase. Those translations (KJV, NKJV) which follow the majority of Greek manuscripts retain this saying. Recent research has shown that there is much evidence that the longer reading of Matthew 19:9 is to be preferred.

Verses 10–12 are contextually related to what Jesus had previously stated in verses 4–9. They give strong support that Jesus was teaching a higher standard than the scribes and the Pharisees. The disciples had an astonished reaction to the teaching of Jesus on the subject of divorce and remarriage. They realized that the permanence of marriage meant a man might be better off not to marry. If Jesus had allowed remarriage for cases of *porneia* He would have simply been agreeing with the conservative school of Shammai. The response of the disciples confirms that man was in a serious situation. He could not be freed from a marriage, even if his wife was guilty of *porneia*.

In response to their reaction Jesus assures them that they would be able to accept such a high standard. Jesus uses the illustration of eunuchs to prove what He has just commanded. Some are born eunuchs. Some are made eunuchs by other men. Some voluntarily make themselves eunuchs for the sake of the kingdom of heaven. Since eunuchs are able to refrain from sexual relations then His followers would be able to refrain from remarriage. The true disciple of Christ will be given the grace to obey what God has commanded.

Summary

No legislation or cultural pressure exists in modern Western society which would compel a man to divorce his wife if she was guilty of *porneia*. Jesus told His disciples to forgive seventy times seven. Men are commanded to love their wives as Christ loved the Church. If a man's wife is found to have been unfaithful love and forgiveness are God's standards, not divorce. If one spouse deserts the other to live in an adulteress relationship, the one flesh bond may be polluted but still remains intact. Since the one flesh bond is never truly broken by anything except death or the rapture, remarriage after divorce is considered adultery.

Grammatical Study

Grammar and syntax regulate the formation and usage of words in a sentence. They come from analyzing and classifying the language itself. They do not externally govern the language; they simply deal with the internal facts of how the language is constructed. Grammar and syntax tell us how words relate to one another in any given sentence. Lexicons give the possible range of meanings for a particular word. Grammar and syntax tell us how each word is used in a particular sentence. The syntactical relations and groupings of words are factors just as important for the bearing of significance as the lexicographical aspect of a single word.

The main grammatical issue appears in Matthew 19:9. A person can get an adequate understanding of the issues involved by comparing several good English translations of the Bible. A better grasp can be attained by looking at the sentence structure in Greek.

Matthew 19:9 states, "And I say to you, whoever divorces his wife, except *porneia*, and marries another, commits adultery."

Which clause(s) does the phrase "except *porneia*" modify? Some claim the phrase "except *porneia*" modifies the following verb phrase "and marries another" as well as the preceding "whoever divorces his wife." In saying this they wish to prove that the person who divorces for the cause of *porneia* does not commit adultery if he remarries.

One commentator writes:

> Although it is not directly stated it seems obvious from the words of our Lord that where a divorce has been obtained on grounds of adultery, the innocent party is free to remarry.[6]

D. A. Carson in his book *Exegetical Fallacies* calls this the "abuse of obviously." He writes:

> It is perfectly proper for a commentator to use "obviously" when he or she has marshaled such overwhelming evidence that the vast majority of readers would concur that the matter being presented

6. William MacDonald, *Believer's Bible Commentary*, Matt. 19:9.

is transparent, or that the argument is logically conclusive. But it is improper to use such expressions when opposing arguments have not been decisively refuted, and it is a fallacy to think the expressions themselves add anything substantial to the argument.[7]

The previously quoted commentator makes the mistake of inserting the word adultery in place of fornication. He then fails to decisively refute or even mention opposing arguments regarding Matthew 19:9. He does not deal with lexical, grammatical, or exegetical evidence. He simply gives his opinion on this subject. He openly admits that what he is teaching is not directly stated. This is unwise. If it is not directly stated in Matthew 19:9, then it is not stated anywhere in the entire New Testament.

There are grammatical problems with claiming *porneia* allows a person to remarry as well as divorce. 'Except *porneia*' is a prepositional phrase. It does not contain a verb. One must be supplied from somewhere else in the sentence. Prepositional phrases are adverbial and normally qualify the verb which they follow. Matthew 19:9 contains a compound conditional clause (two verbal actions).

Matthew placed "except *porneia*" after the first verbal action, "divorce." Like this: Whoever divorces his wife, except *porneia*, and marries another, commits adultery.

In this case 'except *porneia*' modifies only the preceding verbal action, divorce. This construction allows divorce for the cause of *porneia* but not remarriage. This is where it is placed in the Greek text.

He could have placed "except *porneia*" after the second verbal action, "and marries another." Like this: Whoever divorces his wife and marries another, except *porneia*, commits adultery.

In this case "except *porneia*" would modify two sequential actions, divorce and remarriage. This construction would allow remarriage if the divorce occurred for the cause of *porneia*.

Summary

The syntactical burden of proof lies on those who claim that the clause "except *porneia*" modifies the following verbal action "marries", as well as the preceding verb "divorces." The grammatical evidence points to Jesus only allowing a very restrictive form of divorce without the right to remarry. The early church writers (many used Greek as their mother tongue) interpreted the "exception clause" to allow only divorce, not remarriage. The Reformers did not claim the exception clause modifies "and marries

7. D. A. Carson, *Exegetical Fallacies*, p. 122.

another," they resorted to legal fiction. If the exception clause modifies "marriage" as well as "divorce," it would seem strange that the early Christians who spoke Greek would not recognize this.

Bill Heth writes:

> The syntactical argument that except fornication modifies remarriage as well as divorce is unique to the latter half of this [the 20th] century. The early church Fathers understood the exception clause as a simple limitation of the divorce action only, not a "dissolution" of marriage. They never discuss or debate the modern day controversy about which verb or verbs the exception clause qualifies [brackets mine].[8]

The grammatical evidence shows that Matthew's construction was not meant to qualify both the following, as well as the preceding, verbal action. If it was, then this would be the only place in the entire New Testament where such a grammatical construction appears.

Logical Interpretation

God has given man a logical mind. Logic alone is fallible. Logic guided by the constraints of Scripture can help determine if one's arguments and conclusions are consistent with all the biblical data. Those who claim Matthew 19:9 allows a divorced person freedom to remarry create logical fallacies which are inconsistent with all the biblical evidence.

1. Those who allow remarriage usually maintain that *porneia* is a one-to-one equivalent for adultery in Matthew 5:32 and 19:9. They then claim this adultery breaks the one flesh bond and allows a person to remarry without committing adultery. No biblical passage clearly teaches the *one flesh* marriage bond is ever broken by anything except death. Those who claim the *one flesh* bond is broken by adultery must contend with inconsistency. If a man's wife commits adultery then the two would cease to be *one flesh*. The man who continued to live with his wife after she committed adultery would be having sexual relations with a woman whom he had ceased to be *one flesh* with. Consistency would require the couple in this instance to remarry in order to restore the *one flesh* bond. If the wife committed adultery a second time, the process would need to be repeated all over again. Some have taught that it is persistent or continual adultery, not a single act that breaks the *one flesh* bond and allows a person the freedom to divorce and remarry. This is also illogical. One act of adultery either

8. William Heth, *May a Divorced Person Remarry?* p. 3.

does or does not dissolve the marriage bond. There can be no middle ground.

2. Some teach that Matthew 19:9 allows only the "innocent" spouse freedom to remarry in cases of adultery. This is inconsistent as well as illogical. If adultery truly breaks the marriage bond then both parties would be free to remarry; not just the "innocent" one. This teaching would put a premium on the sin of adultery. A person who wanted a divorce could commit adultery (or claim they had) in order to be released from their marriage. If a person claimed to have committed adultery there would be no way to prove that they had not.

3. Matthew 5:32 teaches that the man who divorces his wife for any reason except *porneia* causes her to commit adultery. A man could put away his wife for reasons other than *porneia* and simply wait. Once she remarried (committed adultery) the Erasmian interpretation of Matthew 19:9 would allow the husband freedom to remarry without himself committing adultery. The man who caused his wife's adultery would be the one who was allowed to remarry. The woman who was unjustly put away would not be allowed to remarry without committing adultery. Consistent application of the Erasmian position would allow a man to divorce his wife for *any reason* and remarry without committing adultery. The Early Church, Betrothal, and Incestuous positions cause no such problems.

Conclusion

The lexical, grammatical, exegetical, and logical evidence points to the 'exception clause' as allowing divorce only in the limited instance of *porneia*. Jesus was not compelling people to divorce an adulterous spouse. Man's legal bill of divorcement could never separate what God had joined together (Matt. 19:6). He was not telling divorced people to remarry. This would be in opposition to God's *one flesh* covenant (Matt. 19:5). This is why the disciples were so astonished at the teaching of Jesus (Matt. 19:10). They knew Christ was teaching a higher standard than the religious leaders of His day (Matt. 5:20, 7:28–29).

Lehman Straus writes:

> The whole idea of divorce is diametrically opposed to the marriage plan as it was instituted by God . . . Beware of all teaching and teachers, whether in or out of the organized church, which speak of "scriptural grounds for divorce."[9]

9. Lehman Strauss, *The Permanency of the Marriage Relationship.*

No plain rendered statement in the entire New Testament clearly mandates the right of a divorced person to remarry while their spouse is alive. Matthew 19:9 may come closest, but the 'exception clause' gives an exception for divorce which does not include the right to remarry. Jesus taught that the permanence of marriage was based on the *one flesh* bond which God had ordained for man and woman from the beginning of creation. It is for this reason that man is not to separate what God has joined together.

Mark 10

> And the Pharisees came to him, and asked him, Is it lawful for a man to put away his wife? Tempting him. And he answered and said unto them, What did Moses command you? And they said, Moses suffered to write a bill of divorcement, and to put her away. And Jesus answered and said unto them, For hardness of your heart he wrote you this precept. But from the beginning of the creation God made them male and female. For this cause shall a man leave his father and mother, and cleave to his wife; And they twain shall be one flesh: so then they are no more twain, but one flesh. What therefore God hath joined together, let not man put asunder. And in the house his disciples asked him again of the same matter. And he saith unto them, Whosoever shall put away his wife, and marry another, committeth adultery against her. And if a woman shall put away her husband, and be married to another, she committeth adultery. (Mark 10:2–12)

It was now the spring of Jesus' final year of ministry. He had just left Capernaum, went through Judea, and ended up on the east side of the Jordan in Perea. Perea was one of two districts under the jurisdiction of Herod Antipas. Herod Antipas had previously thrown John the Baptist in prison for preaching against his divorce and remarriage. It was under these circumstances that the Pharisees came to ask Jesus a test question concerning divorce.

The Pharisees asked Jesus whether it was lawful for a man to divorce his wife? Jesus said to them, "What did Moses command you?" The Pharisees believed that Moses permitted a man to divorce his wife if he protected her rights by giving her a certificate of divorce. First century Rabbinic law not only allowed divorce it *compelled* it. A man was not permitted to be reconciled to a fornicating wife.

In verse 5 Jesus claimed that it was their hard-heartedness and obstinate refusal to accept God's view of marriage that allowed for divorce.

The Law of Moses only acknowledged the presence of divorce; it did not institute or authorize it. Jesus took his tempters back to God's original divine intent regarding the institution of marriage. The man and woman are not simply two partners in a legal contract. They are joined together in an indissoluble *one flesh* covenant union. Because of this, what God has joined together let no man separate.

Later, while the disciples and Jesus were in a house, the disciples asked him for a confirmation of what he had previously spoken. Although Jesus spoke to the religious leaders in proverbs he answered the disciple's questions in a straight forward manner: "The man who divorces his wife and remarries commits adultery." Both Matthew 19 and Mark 10 give a synopsis of the same event. Each author was inspired by the Holy Spirit to record those items which would be needed by their intended audience. Matthew wrote primarily for Jewish readers and recorded the *exception* for divorce in the case of fornication. This was probably included because of the Rabbinic law which compelled a man to divorce his fornicating wife. Mark wrote to a Roman audience. He included Jesus' teaching regarding a woman who divorced her husband and remarried. He gave no exception for divorce. Even though Roman law compelled a man to divorce an adulterous wife, it did not allow her to remarry. The *lex Iulia de pudicitia et coercendis adulteriis*—"The Julian law of chastity and repressing adultery" —was established by Augustus and the Roman Senate in 18 BC.

Concerning this law Will Durant writes:

> Within sixty days of detecting a wife's adultery, the husband was required to bring her before the court; if he failed to do this, the woman's father was required to indict her; if he too failed, any citizen might accuse her. The adulterous woman was to be banished for life, was to lose a third of her fortune and half her dowry, and must not marry again.[10]

Under Roman law a woman could initiate a divorce. Rabbinic law did not allow this. Though Roman law allowed remarriage after divorce in most cases, Jesus boldly claimed that whoever remarries after divorcing their spouse commits adultery.

Luke 16

> And the Pharisees also, who were covetous, heard all these things: and they derided him. And he said unto them, Ye are they which

---

10. Will Durant, *Caesar and Christ*, p. 223.

justify yourselves before men; but God knows your hearts: for that which is highly esteemed among men is abomination in the sight of God. The law and the prophets were until John: since that time the kingdom of God is preached, and every man presses into it. And it is easier for heaven and earth to pass, than one tittle of the law to fail. Whosoever putteth away his wife, and marrieth another, committeth adultery: and whosoever marrieth her that is put away from her husband committeth adultery. (Luke 16:14–18)

The Pharisees scoffed at Jesus for teaching man cannot serve both God and money. Their covetousness was detestable to God. They had nullified the true interpretation of the Law and the Prophets. They had justified their actions by living according to the traditions of men. Jesus announced that since John the Baptist, the kingdom of God had been preached. The coming of the New Covenant did not set aside God's law; rather it was the fulfillment of it. It would be easier for heaven and earth to pass away than for the smallest part of the law to fail. The Old Testament prophecies would be completely fulfilled, and the moral law of God would remain absolutely authoritative. The Pharisees were very adept at setting aside the true meaning of God's law and inventing their own standards of righteousness (cf. Mark 7:13).

In verse 18 Jesus uses an illustration to show the Pharisees how far they were from obeying the true intent of God's law. He tells them that *everyone* who divorces his wife and marries another commits adultery. The man who marries the divorced woman also commits adultery. The Pharisees allowed both remarriage after divorce. The evidence shows Jesus did not. Man may attempt to justify himself by lowering God's standards and then judging himself accordingly. God knows the hearts of everyone. In the end, all judgment will be based upon God's impeccable righteousness.

Conclusion

Jesus based His teaching concerning marriage on the one flesh union created by God. His standards were permanence and forgiveness. Though realizing culture may compel one to put away a fornicating spouse, He never commanded divorce. Divorce was caused by hardness of heart (Mark 10:5). Hardness of heart may lead one partner to commit adultery. Hardness of heart may cause a spouse to be unforgiving. Neither are God's will. If adultery occurs, it does not dissolve the one flesh bond or replace it with a new one. If a legal divorce takes place, it cannot nullify the one flesh relationship which exists between husband and wife.

Heth and Wenham write:

> Should a man be forced to put away his unfaithful wife, as the
> Jewish readers of Matthew's Gospel would have been, Jesus does
> not hold him responsible for breaking His command not to di-
> vorce. The guilt and the blame lie with the woman who is an adul-
> teress by reason of her offense. And should the hard-heartedness
> of one of the partners result in an unfortunate divorce, lack of
> forgiveness and a refusal to be reconciled, Jesus requires His dis-
> ciples to remain single. One thing appears certain from this study:
> the New Testament and the early church as a whole are not vague
> or confusing when it comes to the question of remarriage after
> divorce. It is clear that Jesus said that a man may have one wife
> or no wife, and if someone puts away their partner for whatever
> reason, they must remain single.[11]

Jesus did not command people to divorce a fornicating spouse. He
told them to forgive. He did not tell divorced people to remarry. He told
them to reconcile or remain single (1 Cor. 7:11).

---

11 Heth and Wenham, *Jesus and Divorce*, p. 199.

Chapter 3

The Epistles

Romans 7

> Know ye not, brethren, (for I speak to them that know the law) how that the law hath dominion over a man as long as he lives? For the woman which hath an husband is bound by the law to her husband so long as he lives; but if the husband be dead, she is loosed from the law of her husband. So then if, while her husband lives, she be married to another man, she shall be called an adulteress: but if her husband be dead, she is free from the law; so that she is no adulteress, though she be married to another man. (Rom. 7:1–3)

VERSES 1–3 relate back to Romans 6:14. In Romans 6:14 Paul states the believer is not under law but under grace. Though Paul's primary concern is to show the believer's release from the law, the illustration he uses sheds light on the permanence of marriage. The law of marriage binds a woman to her husband as long as he lives. No exceptions! Only when her husband dies is she free to remarry. If a woman marries another man while her husband is alive she shall be called an adulteress. "Shall be called" is in the future tense. A good rendering of this would be "she shall from this time on, be known as an adulteress." The widow who remarries is not an adulteress. When a woman's husband dies, she is free from the law of marriage.

Paul is neither contradicting nor adding to the teaching of Christ. He is reaffirming the one flesh concept of marriage that is expressed throughout the Bible. Marriage is a permanent kinship bond that can only be broken by death. This is one of the clearest passages on the permanence of marriage. Not surprisingly some have gone out of their way to say Paul wasn't teaching about divorce and remarriage at all. The argument usually given is that Paul was teaching a widow has the right to remarry.

Paul's main intention is to teach the believer's release from the law. He uses what is known (the permanence of marriage) to illustrate what he wishes to teach (the believer's release from the law). The woman, whose husband has died, is free to remarry. The woman who remarries while her husband is alive is an adulteress. Neither is the main point of the passage. Nevertheless, both are true. One cannot be chosen without the other.

First Corinthians 6

> Know ye not that your bodies are the members of Christ? Shall I then take the members of Christ, and make them the members of a harlot? God forbid. What? know ye not that he which is joined to a harlot is one body? for two, says He, shall become one flesh. But he that is joined unto the Lord is one spirit. Flee fornication. Every sin that a man doeth is without the body: but he that commits fornication sins against his own body. (1 Cor. 6:15–18)

First Corinthians 6 does not speak concerning marriage, divorce, or remarriage. Nevertheless, some have attempted to use this text to teach adultery dissolves or creates a second *one flesh* bond. Some even claim the man who commits fornication with a harlot is married to her. The context of this passage speaks of the believer's oneness and union with Christ. The believer is to flee fornication because his body is a member of Christ.

One significant observation is that the text does not mention whether the believer is married or not. *Porneia* might include adultery but may simply refer to sexual relations before one is married. Even if it could be assumed the believer was married, nothing is stated about the dissolution of marriage by fornication. If it is believed that fornication dissolves a marriage, it would be more consistent with the text to say this fornication could also wed the man to the harlot. Every time a man committed fornication he would cease to be married to his current wife and be wed to the harlot.

The text states that the man is "one body" (*soma*/4983) with the harlot not "one flesh" (*sarka*/4561). There is a difference. The first speaks of being united in an illegitimate physical relationship with a harlot and no more. The second speaks of being united in a legitimate physical, emotional, and possibly even spiritual relationship with one's wife. The context speaks of the believer being united with Christ, not with his wife. The believer who unites himself to a harlot is, in a sense, *one body* with her. Yet this does not mean he is married to her. True biblical marriage is more than a sexual act.

The believer who commits fornication mars, but does not end, the unique relationship he has with Christ.

First Corinthians 7 General Outline

In First Corinthians 7 Paul deals with marriage and issues related to it. Paul addresses different groups of people and gives guiding principles and instructions for each situation. Difficulties arise when people interpret this chapter without first examining the context and identifying structural markers and transitions.

Chapter 7 has two main divisions. Paul uses the structural marker "now concerning" (*peri de*) to address two different groups. Verses 1–24 give directions to married couples and those who were previously married, i.e., widows, widowers, and divorcees. Verses 25–38 address those who were never previously married, i.e. virgins and bachelors. Paul gives advice concerning their betrothal or engagement.

> 7:1–7 Paul instructs married couples to fulfill their conjugal duties to one another.
>
> 7:8–9 Paul directs widows and the unmarried (possibly a reference to widowers) concerning self control. It would be good for them to remain unmarried, but for those who burn with passion it is better to marry.
>
> 7:10–11 Both the Lord and Paul taught the permanence of marriage for all people. Believers in particular are not to divorce. If a divorce occurs, they are to remain single or be reconciled.
>
> 7:12–16 Jesus Christ left no specific teaching in the gospels for believers who are married to unbelievers. Paul instructs believers to be at peace with their unbelieving partner.
>
> 7:17–24 Believers should remain in the same condition they were in when saved. External circumstances and human masters are of secondary importance to spiritual life and the Lordship of Christ.
>
> 7:25–38 Paul instructs those who were previously unmarried (virgins), concerning marriage and betrothal.
>
> 7:39–40 Concluding remarks on the law of marriage.

First Corinthians 7

> Now concerning the things whereof ye wrote unto me: It is good for a man not to touch a woman. Nevertheless, to avoid fornication, let every man have his own wife, and let every woman have her own husband. Let the husband render unto the wife due benevolence: and likewise also the wife unto the husband. The wife hath not power of her own body, but the husband: and likewise also the husband hath not power of his own body, but the wife. Defraud ye not one the other, except it be with consent for a time, that ye may give yourselves to fasting and prayer; and come together again, that Satan tempt you not for incontinency. But I speak this by permission, and not of commandment. For I would that all men were even as I myself. But every man hath his proper gift of God, one after this manner, and another after that. (1 Cor. 7:1–7)

Verse 1 The Corinthians had previously written to Paul and made the statement: "It is good for a man not to touch a woman." Paul gives his reply in verses 2–7. The NIV translates this verse "it is good for a man not to marry." This is an interpretation rather than a translation. It is also a doubtful meaning of the verse. It is more probable that the Corinthians had questioned Paul concerning the practice of celibacy within the confines of marriage. The term "to touch" is used in Classical Greek and the Septuagint as a figurative expression for sexual intercourse (cf. Gen. 20:6).

Chrysostom writes in his *Homilies on First Corinthians 7*:

> Wherefore he says, "Now concerning the things whereof ye wrote unto me." For they had written to him, "Whether it was right to abstain from one's wife, or not:" and writing back in answer to this and giving rules about marriage, he also introduces the discourse concerning virginity: "It is good for a man not to touch a woman."

Although he allows Paul to introduce the topic of virginity, Chrysostom realizes the Corinthians main question regarded the practice of celibacy within the confines of marriage.

Verse 2 Fornication, or sexual immorality, was rampant in Corinth. Because of this, each man was to *have* his own wife and each wife was to *have* her own husband. The context of the passage and its relationship to verses 1–7 suggests the word "have" does not mean single people should get married. Rather, it means that married people should continue to perform their conjugal duties. Paul uses *have* as an expression for sexual intercourse in First Corinthians 5:1 as well.

Verse 3 The husband is to give to his wife the affection due her and also the wife to her husband. *Affection* speaks of the conjugal duties performed for the benefit of both spouses.

Verse 4 When two people marry, they become *one flesh*. A married person actually belongs to their spouse. Individual rights cease in the bond of marriage. The man who loves his wife, is actually loving himself (cf. Eph. 5:28).

Verse 5 Depriving one's spouse without consent is fraud. Paul gives four stipulations for couples who wish to abstain from sexual relations. 1) It must be for a designated period of time. 2) It must be mutually agreed upon before hand. 3) It must be for the purpose of devoting oneself to fasting and prayer. 4) At the end of this period the couples must resume sexual relations. This is to thwart Satan's temptations because of their lack of self control.

Verse 6 Paul's concession allows married Christians permission to abstain from sexual intercourse for a given period of time. Paul does not want the statement given in verse 5 to be misconstrued as a command. A couple is allowed or permitted to abstain from sexual relations for the purpose of fasting and prayer. They are not commanded to do so. It would also be acceptable to fast and pray while continuing in normal sexual relations.

Verse 7 Paul wished that all men could live as he did. Because Paul was unmarried He was able to continually practice celibacy and totally devote his life to Christ. There is nothing intrinsically spiritual about being single. The benefit is the freedom it gives to serve Christ rather than one's spouse. Paul also recognized that some men are given different gifts by the Holy Spirit. The word used here for "gift" is (*charisma*/5486). It is the same word used in First Corinthians 12 and Romans 12 for spiritual gifts. Singleness is a gift from God, marriage is also.

First Corinthians 7:8–9

> I say therefore to the unmarried and widows, It is good for them if they abide even as I. But if they cannot contain, let them marry: for it is better to marry than to burn.

Verse 8 Paul wishes that the unmarried and widows could remain as he was. Namely, maintaining a state of continual celibacy which gives freedom to serve Christ. The word widow here is feminine. It means a woman who was previously married but whose husband has now died. Some assemblies maintained an official list of widows for those who were to receive financial assistance from the local assembly. Only those women who were over sixty years of age and met other criteria were to be put on the list. Younger widows were to remarry and bear children rather than burn with lust (cf. 1 Tim. 5). Paul felt it would be good for widows to remain single, but also understood if they did not.

The definition of the term unmarried (*agamois*/22) is of some debate. Some believe it means bachelors or those men who have never been married. The word is in the masculine gender. It is also possible that unmarried includes widowers, as well as bachelors. In context however, it may simply mean widowers. In verses 1–24 Paul seems to be dealing only with those who were married or previously married. Paul deals with bachelors and virgins in verses 25–38. Paul uses the word *unmarried* in a parallel structure with the word widow (*cherais*/5503). There is a word in the Greek for widower (*cheros*), but it is not used in the New Testament or Septuagint. *Liddell and Scott's Greek-English Lexicon* states the word "unmarried" can denote bachelors or widowers. Paul does not deal with single people until the end of chapter 7 so it is doubtful he would use the word in this verse to refer to men who have never been married.

A side note here needs to be dealt with. Those who cross reference verse 8 with verse 11 to prove that a divorcee may remarry are simply not interpreting contextually. Paul plainly states that the *unmarried* in verse 11 are people who are legally separated or divorced from their spouse. For them they are to remain single or be reconciled. The word unmarried (*agamos*/22) is used only four times in the New Testament. All of them occur in First Corinthians 7. In verse 8 Paul uses the word to refer to bachelors or widowers. In verse 11 it means those who are legally divorced. In verses 32 and 34 unmarried speaks of both men and women who have never married. A word may have different nuances which fall within its semantic range but its exact meaning is best determined by its use in context.

Another issue related to verse 8 is whether Paul was a bachelor or a widower. In favor of him being a bachelor is that no place in Scripture is there any mention of Paul having a wife or children. In favor of Paul being a widower are the following. A) Unmarried rabbis were few and far between. The Mishnah appears to make marriage obligatory for all Jewish men except those who were impotent. B) Some believe Paul was a member of the Sanhedrin and therefore must have been married. Acts 26:10 may simply mean Paul agreed with the Sanhedrin, not that he was a member of it. C) If contextually, "unmarried" means widowers in verse 8, then it would make Paul's statement, "it is good for them to remain even as I am," even more consistent. Unless further evidence is unearthed, we cannot be sure whether Paul was a bachelor or widower. All we know is that at the time of his writings Paul was *unmarried* and abiding in a state of celibacy.

Verse 9 If these unmarried men and widows do not have control over their own passions they should get married. This is the same advice that Paul gave widows in First Timothy 5:11–12. The word "burn" here means to inwardly be on fire. An inward struggle is in view here that could be fatal to ones peace and sanctification.

First Corinthians 7:10–11

> And unto the married I command, yet not I, but the Lord, Let not the wife depart from her husband: but if she depart, let her remain unmarried, or be reconciled to her husband: and let not the husband put away his wife.

Verse 10 Paul now transitions from those who are unmarried and may want to marry to those who are married and may want out. What he states here is not a concession or even his opinion. It is a direct command from the Lord. The Lord gave specific directions in the gospels regarding the permanence of marriage.

F. F. Bruce comments:

> For a Christian husband, or wife, divorce is excluded by the law of Christ: here Paul has no need to express a judgment of his own, for the Lord's ruling on this matter was explicit.[1]

Some see verses 10–11 as teaching that the permanence of marriage applies only to a believer who is married to another believer. They claim that verses 12–16 allow a believer who is deserted by an unbeliever to divorce and remarry. It is said that the permanence of marriage does not apply in the case of a believer being deserted by an unbeliever.

It is doubtful that Paul is limiting his statement in verses 10–11 only to believers. A better and more consistent understanding of this section seems to be that verses 10–11 give the general teaching of Christ regarding the permanence of marriage as applied to believers who are married to one another. In verses 12–16 Paul applies the doctrine of the permanence of marriage to believers who are married to unbelievers. The believer is to allow the unbeliever to depart, but after that the believer is to remain

---

1. F. F. Bruce, *Paul: Apostle of the Heart Set Free*, p. 267.

unmarried or be reconciled. Why? The one flesh bond exists between two people regardless of whether one, both, or neither are believers.

Paul claimed that he was teaching what Christ taught on divorce and remarriage. It is doubtful that Paul was speaking of a special revelation he had received from the Lord regarding a believer who was married to another believer. If this was so, why didn't Paul also receive a revelation concerning believers who were married to unbelievers? The more probable scenario is that this was Paul's inspired understanding of Christ's teaching concerning divorce and remarriage as recorded in the gospels. Jesus left no specific teaching concerning marriage between two believers or between a believer and an unbeliever. Rather, Christ spoke about the permanence of marriage for all people whether they were believers or not. Jesus preached to the mixed multitudes, unbelieving Pharisees, and His disciples. Since the *one flesh* covenant of marriage is rooted in the creation ordinance of Genesis 1 and 2 Christ made no delineation that the marriage bond was permanent between two believers but not between a believer and an unbeliever.

Verse 11 Though Christ's will is no divorce, the Bible recognizes that divorces do occur. The divorce here is the woman's act, not her husbands. If she no longer wishes to remain with her husband, she has only two options: return to her husband or remain single. Marrying another man is not a biblical option.

The woman is probably not just separated from her husband, but legally divorced. Paul uses two terms (*chorizo*/5562) and (*aphiemi*/863) interchangeably to refer to divorce (cf. vs. 15). He realizes that according to Roman law, the woman was allowed to remarry. The law of Christ prohibits such an action.

Paul states that the Lord commanded the husband not to divorce his wife. Fornication is not listed as an exception for divorce. The Corinthian Christians were not coerced by Jewish customs to put away a fornicating wife. Christ allowed divorce in this one instance because of the hardness of man's heart. Paul had no need to make mention of this allowance. The biblical pattern is forgiveness, not divorce.

First Corinthians 7:12–16

> But to the rest speak I, not the Lord: if any brother hath a wife that believeth not, and she be pleased to dwell with him, let him not put her away. And the woman which hath an husband that believeth not, and if he be pleased to dwell with her, let her not leave him. For the unbelieving husband is sanctified by the wife, and

the unbelieving wife is sanctified by the husband; else were your children unclean: but now they are holy. But if the unbelieving depart, let him depart. A brother or a sister is not under bondage in such cases: but God hath called us to peace. For what knowest thou, O wife, whether thou shalt save thy husband? Or knowest thou, O man, whether thou shalt save thy wife?

Verse 12 Paul now shifts to a particular group of believers; those who have come to faith in Christ after being married, but their spouse has not. "I, not the Lord" does not mean this statement is uninspired or any less authoritative. Paul is merely stating that the gospels record no specific teaching by Christ concerning a believer who is married to an unbeliever. If a believing man has an unbelieving wife who consents to live with him, he should not divorce her.

Verse 13 If a believing woman has an unbelieving husband who consents to live with her, she should not divorce him.

Verse 14 The believing spouse in a mixed marriage is "holy" or set apart unto the Lord. By way of relationship through the covenant of marriage the unbelieving spouse, as well as the children, are sanctified. Not that unbelieving partners or children are automatically saved, but that the marriage between the believer and the unbeliever is holy and approved by God. The believing spouse sanctifies the home and gives the children a Christian influence they would not otherwise have.

Verse 15 If the unbelieving partner wishes to depart, the Christian is to let them. God has called His children to live in peace with all men. This includes one's spouse. The believing spouse is to love their partner and allow them to stay. If this fails, they are not in bondage to preserve a working relationship.

In Romans 7:2 and First Corinthians 7:39 Paul teaches that the wife is bound to her husband as long as he lives. In First Corinthians 7:27 he claims the betrothed man is bound to his wife. The word in these three passages is (*deo*/1210). It means to tie or to bind. In First Corinthians 7:15 Paul uses a different and unrelated word (*douloo*/1402). It means to be enslaved. The Bible never uses the word "enslaved" to refer to the marriage relationship. Many have attempted to read into this verse that a deserted spouse is free to remarry.

One commentator errs when he writes:

> Paul did not say as he did in verse 11, that the Christian in this case should remain unmarried.[2]

2. David Lowery, *First Corinthians*, p. 518

This is an argument from silence. Jesus claimed fornication was the only grounds allowed for divorce and nowhere stated that the 'innocent' spouse was free to remarry. Paul understood what the Lord had commanded and would not be led by the Spirit to teach otherwise. Paul never once stated that the Christian in this instance was free to remarry. Would it truly be necessary for Paul to reiterate that a spouse was to remain single or be reconciled, when he had already done so four verses earlier? Paul twice writes that the married woman remains bound to her husband as long as he lives; not until adultery, not until desertion, but until death.

The best interpretation of First Corinthians 7:15 is that the believer is not enslaved to keep the unbeliever from departing. The Christian is exempt from the responsibility for the divorce which the unbelieving partner initiates. The believer is called to peace and does not need to resort to coercion or legal maneuvers to preserve the relationship.

Robertson and Plummer write:

> We cannot safely argue with Luther that *ou dedoulotai* [not under bondage] implies that the Christian partner, when divorced by the heathen partner, may remarry again. All that *ou dedoulotai* clearly means is that he or she need not feel so bound by Christ's prohibition of divorce as to be afraid to depart when the heathen partner insists on separation [brackets mine].[3]

Paul uses the same word for divorce (*chorizo*/5563) in both verses 11 and 15 to refer to divorce. This shows that we are in the realm of full legal divorce. The laws of men allow remarriage; the laws of Christ do not. This is how early Christian writers interpreted and applied First Corinthians 7:15. They allowed the unbeliever to depart and freed the believer from guilt or liability of divorce. The departure of the spouse did not grant the believer freedom to remarry. The one flesh bond exists between husband and wife whether they are legally divorced or not. The laws of men, and physical proximity of spouses to one another, have no bearing upon the *one flesh* covenant.

Verse 16 The Christian spouse is to allow the unbelieving partner to depart without bearing the responsibility for the unbeliever's actions. There are two primary reasons for living in harmony within this situation. First, there is no way of knowing whether the unbeliever will turn to Christ. Second, the Christian partner may be the channel used by God to save their partner. Until their last dying breath, there remains hope for their salvation. Until they die, there remains hope for reconciliation. Living in a

---

3. Robertson and Plummer, *First Epistle of St. Paul to the Corinthians*, p. 143

state of tension, disharmony, and legal battles with an unbelieving spouse would not display the peace of Christ. It may close off future possibilities for witness and testimony of Christ's love and forgiveness.

First Corinthians 7:17–24

> But as God hath distributed to every man, as the Lord hath called every one, so let him walk. And so ordain I in all the churches. Is any man called being circumcised? Let him not become uncircumcised. Is any called in uncircumcision? Let him not be circumcised. Circumcision is nothing, and uncircumcision is nothing, but the keeping of the commandments of God. Let every man abide in the same calling wherein he was called. Art thou called being a servant? Care not for it: but if thou mayest be made free, use it rather. For he that is called in the Lord, being a servant, is the Lord's freeman: likewise also he that is called, being free, is Christ's servant. Ye are bought with a price; be not ye the servants of men. Brethren, let every man, wherein he is called, therein abide with God.

The main emphasis of verses 17–24 is that believers should remain in the same situation in life in which they were called. Outward physical circumstances are of little concern in the life of the believer. The emphasis is upon Christ as Lord and obeying Him from the heart.

Hodge writes:

> Paul was not only averse to breaking up the conjugal relationship, but it was a general ordinance of His that men should remain in the same social position after becoming Christians, which they had occupied before . . . Paul endeavored to convince his readers that their relation to Christ was compatible with any social relation or position. It mattered not whether they were circumcised or uncircumcised, bond or free, married to a Christian or married to a Gentile, their conversion to Christianity involved, therefore, no necessity of breaking asunder their social ties.[4]

Verses 17–24 are not a digression or an interlude to Paul's train of thought. Rather, they are an extension of it. One's marital status before the Lord is not of primary importance. Paul illustrates this by showing that those who belong to Christ should remain as they were called. This does not mean that those who come to Christ while involved in sexually immoral relationships are free to continue in such. The teaching of

4. Charles Hodge, *Commentary on 1 and 2 Corinthians*, p. 120.

Scripture is that those who come to Christ are expected to change any and all immoral behavior.

First Corinthians 7:25–28

> Now concerning virgins I have no commandment of the Lord: yet I give my judgment, as one that hath obtained mercy of the Lord to be faithful. I suppose therefore that this is good for the present distress, I say, that it is good for a man so to be. Art thou bound unto a wife? Seek not to be loosed. Art thou loosed from a wife? Seek not a wife. But and if thou marry, thou hast not sinned. Nevertheless such shall have trouble in the flesh: but I spare you.

Verse 25 Paul begins with the structural marker "now concerning" (*peri de*) to transition to a different group of people, namely, virgins. A virgin is one who had never before been married. Paul had no specific commands from the Lord regarding virgins and whether they should marry or remain single. Paul received mercy from the Lord and was faithful and trustworthy to give the Corinthians Spirit-led guidance on this issue.

Verse 26 Paul spoke of the present distress that would make it good for a man to remain as he was. This may refer to a present crisis the Corinthians were facing. Martyrdom and persecution would be less difficult for a single person to endure than for a married person who was responsible for a wife and children.

Verse 27 Contextually, those who are bound to a wife may refer to betrothed couples. Paul claims they are virgins yet claims they are bound to a wife. Paul would not call them virgins (*parthenos*/3933) if they had already consummated a marriage. Betrothal was more than being engaged. A betrothed couple was legally married and considered husband and wife even though they had never consummated their marriage (cf. Matt.1:18–25, 2 Cor. 11:2). Once betrothed, a legal divorce was necessary to be released from the marriage. Here Paul applies the same principle to virgins as he does to others; remain as you were called.

Those who had entered into a betrothal agreement should not seek to be released from it. Those who are released from a betrothal agreement should not seek to enter into one. Paul uses the verb (*deo*/1210) not (*douloo*/1402) to refer to the marriage bond here. He uses the word (*lusin*/3080) to refer to the being released from a wife. Paul uses a different word in verses 11 and 15 to refer to divorce.

Some Erasmian interpreters mistakenly teach that the use of the *Perfect Passive* verb form, instead of the *Present Active*, means that the man who is "loosed from a wife" was divorced and Paul is allowing him to remarry. The *Perfect* is the "present state resulting from past action." There is nothing in the *Perfect* verb form that shows that the man was previously married. There is nothing in the *Perfect* verb form that would lead one to believe the "loosed" man is divorced.

Robertson and Plummer write:

> Here again the perfect means, "Art thou in a state of freedom from matrimonial ties?" It does not mean "Hast thou been freed from a wife by death or divorce?" The verb is chosen because of the preceding *lusin*, and bachelors as well as widowers are addressed.[5]

Grosheide writes:

> *Art thou loosed* need not refer to a marriage which had been previously dissolved by divorce or by the death of the spouse. It may not mean anything more than unmarried.[6]

Paul has already stated that the divorced person is not to remarry. The Bible does not contradict itself. The New Testament contains clear statements that remarriage after divorce is adultery. It is unwise to take a statement out of context and use it to teach something that is refuted elsewhere.

Verse 28 Paul has just told the Corinthian men that they should not seek a wife. This is his advice but he assures those who have already done so that they "have not sinned." Those who do marry, bachelor or virgin, have done nothing wrong. Paul's instruction is not to limit their freedom in Christ or to downgrade marriage. His heart is to spare them troubles in this life.

First Corinthians 7:29–35

> But this I say, brethren, the time is short: it remaineth, that both they that have wives be as though they had none; And they that weep, as though they wept not; and they that buy, as though they possessed not; And they that use this world, as not abusing it: for the fashion of this world passeth away. But I would have you without carefulness. He that is unmarried careth for the things that belong to the Lord, how he may please the Lord: But he that is married careth for the things that are of the world, how he may please his wife. There is a difference also between a wife and a

5. Robertson and Plummer, p. 153.
6. F. W. Grosheide, *First Epistle to the Corinthians*, p. 176.

virgin. The unmarried woman careth for the things of the Lord, that she may be holy both in body and in spirit; but she that is married careth for the things of the world, how she may please her husband. And this I speak for your own profit; not that I may cast a snare upon you, but for that which is comely, and that ye may attend upon the Lord without distraction.

Verses 29–31 Since the return of the Lord is near, the believer should not become engrossed in human relationships or day to day activities such as mourning, rejoicing, buying, or selling. The world is temporary and one's life should be devoted to Christ. Christians can use the world but they must not become permanently attached to it. Those who become overly absorbed in the things of the world are misusing it.

Verse 32 Paul's emphasis was not on remaining single. *Singleness* in and of itself is of no benefit. The benefit of singleness is that it allows one to be free to be more fully devoted to Christ.

Verses 33–34 The married person is under divine command to care for their spouse. Once a man is married his devotion is divided between his wife and Christ. The virgin, or unmarried woman, is free to care about the things of the Lord. This is the difference that exists between the married woman and the virgin. The unmarried woman is free to be holy to the Lord. Being single does not make one pure or holy. Holy here means to be set apart unto Christ. The laws of God and His creation are so established that the wife will be concerned about pleasing her husband. In pleasing her husband, the wife is actually obeying and pleasing Christ (cf. Eph. 5:22).

Verse 35 Paul's aim was not to limit a believer's freedom but to allow them to truly be free to serve the Lord without distraction or divided attention. The word translated snare (*broxos*/1029) is better translated as a leash (NKJV). It is not a trap, but a bridle or a restriction.

First Corinthians 7:36–38

But if any man think that he behaveth himself uncomely toward his virgin, if she pass the flower of her age, and need so require, let him do what he will, he sinneth not: let him marry. Nevertheless he that standeth stedfast in his heart, having no necessity, but hath power over his own will, and hath so decreed in his heart that he will keep his virgin, doeth well. So then he that giveth her in marriage doeth well; but he that giveth her not in marriage doeth better.

Verses 36–38 The interpretation of verses 36–38 is of some debate. The issue revolves around the indefinite pronoun "any man" (*tis*/5100) and the pronoun "his" (*autou*/848) in verse 36. Does this man refer to the virgin's father or the betrothed bridegroom? The traditional view has held it means the father of the bride. The view held by some modern day commentators is that it means the bridegroom. The NIV has gone so far as to translate this passage as referring to the bridegroom while giving the traditional interpretation in the margin. It seems best to leave the translation speaking of any man and allowing the reader to decide which view is correct. The strength of the bridegroom view is that it allows for a consistent subject for the verbs used throughout the passage. The weakness of this view is that it requires the words (*gameo*/1060) and (*gamizo*/1061) to be used as synonymous. Lexically, *gameo* means to marry while *gamizo* usually means to give in marriage. The RSV translates the word "virgin" as betrothed in verses 36 and 37. This is an error. The RSV also translates verse 38 "he who marries his betrothed." This is an interpretation, not a correct translation.

In favor of the "father" view is that the context appears to be speaking of a man who is giving his virgin to be married. In the Corinthian culture the decision was not the bride's but the father's. The virgin could only marry with the father's approval. It would be strange to say a bridegroom would "keep his virgin" for the purpose of betrothal is marriage. The choice would still be the father's not the bridegroom's. It would make little sense for a man to enter into a betrothal and then "keep" her from marriage. Keep here does not mean to leave her a virgin but to retain possession of her. If the bridegroom was to "keep his virgin" then he would be living in a permanent state of betrothal without ever consummating the marriage.

Paul seems to be giving advice to the father of the virgin. Paul doesn't mention the girl's desires but places the whole affair in the hands of the father. The father was the one who exercised decision-making authority in regards to family matters. The father may have already purposed in his heart that the daughter would not marry. If there was no "necessity" or "compulsion" from evidence that his daughter would not be able to remain single he would do well to follow his convictions. If he decided she should marry he does well, but if he decided not to let her marry he does better.

First Corinthians 7:39–40

The wife is bound by the law as long as her husband lives: but if her husband be dead, she is at liberty to be married to whom she will; only in the Lord. But she is happier if she so abides, after my judgment: and I think also that I have the Spirit of God.

Verses 39–40 Paul concludes his teaching on marriage and the issues related to it with an admonition restating the permanence of marriage. The marriage bond may have been held in low regard by the pagan Corinthians, but Paul reminds the believers that marriage is permanent until death. When a woman's husband died, she was free to remarry. This was Paul's Spirit-led teaching regarding the permanence of marriage and his inspired understanding of the teaching of Christ in the gospels on this subject. He gives no exceptions for remarriage except the death of the spouse. If the woman's husband died, she was free to remarry only another Christian. Paul's judgment was that she would be happier by remaining single.

Ephesians 5

Wives, submit yourselves unto your own husbands, as unto the Lord. For the husband is head of the wife, even as Christ is the head of the church: and He is the savior of the body. Therefore as the church is subject unto Christ, so let the wives be to their own husbands in everything. Husbands, love your wives, even as also Christ loved the church, and gave himself for it; that he might sanctify and cleanse it with the washing of water by the word, that he might present it to himself a glorious church, not having spot, or wrinkle, or any such thing; but that it should be holy and without blemish. So ought men to love their wives as their own bodies. He that loves his wife loves himself. For no man ever hated his own flesh; but nourishes it and cherishes it, even as the Lord the church: for we are members of his body, of his flesh, and of his bones. For this cause shall a man leave his father and mother, and shall be joined unto his wife, and they two shall be one flesh. This is a great mystery: but I speak concerning Christ and the church. Nevertheless let every one of you in particular so love his wife even as himself; and the wife see that she reverence her husband. (Eph. 5:22–33)

Ephesians 5 teaches how husbands and wives are to treat one another. It also teaches the permanence of marriage based upon the one flesh concept established by God.

Verses 5:22–24 Wives are to be under the authority of their husbands. This does not mean they are inferior. Rather, God has established a divine order in creation. Christ the Son submits Himself to God the

Father. This does not mean He is inferior or less than God. Instead it shows order. Christ is the head of the church. The church is to submit to Christ as its head. In the same way wives are to submit to their husbands.

Verses 5:25–29 Christ loved the church and gave himself up for her. He died on the cross to cleanse and sanctify her. Husbands are to show the same sacrificial love to their wives. The wife is really one body, or one flesh, with her husband. The husband who does not love his wife hates himself. The husband who loves his wife loves himself. The husband who commits adultery has failed not only to submit to Christ, but also to love his wife. The husband who will not forgive an adulterous wife fails to love her as Christ loved the church. Those who divorce their wives for the reason of sexual immorality are not loving their wives as Christ loved the church.

Verses 5:30–33 The church consists of the members of Christ's body. In verse 31 Paul cites Genesis 2:24 to show how inseparable the church is from Christ. He uses marriage as an illustration of Christ and the church. This covenant bond that binds Christ to the church is the same type of bond that exists between husband and wife. This is evidence against the claim that a marriage may be dissolved by sin. Not even continual persistent adultery can sever the one flesh covenant. The man whose wife lives in this manner is bound by the law of Christ to forgive her and receive her back. Anything less, is to disobey the commands of Scripture. A man is to love his wife as Christ loved the church. Christ will not break his covenant with the members of his body, the church (cf. Heb. 13:5; Matt. 28:20; John 10:28; Rom. 8:35–39; II Cor. 1:22; Eph. 1:13–14).

Since the bond between Christ and His church cannot be broken, neither can the bond be broken between husband and wife. If the marriage bond can be dissolved or severed, then Paul, under divine inspiration of the Holy Spirit, has made a serious mistake by comparing marriage to Christ and the church. The symbolic purpose of Christian marriage is to show the world the type of love Christ has for His church.

Those who claim the right to divorce a sinful spouse have missed the spirit of the New Testament. Those who forgive and receive a wayward spouse are an illustration of the love, forgiveness, and oneness Christ has with His church.

Conclusion

If Christ did allow remarriage after divorce, Paul seems not to know of it. Paul teaches the permanence of marriage with no exceptions. He states the woman is bound to her husband as long as he lives (Rom. 7:2; I Cor.

7:39). If a woman remarries while her husband is alive, she will be called an adulteress (Rom. 7:3). If a woman separates from her husband, she is either to remain single or be reconciled (I Cor. 7:11).

The only allowance Paul makes is that if the unbeliever deserts a believer, the believer is not enslaved. The word used here is entirely different and unrelated to the word Paul uses for the marriage bond. Paul sees the one flesh permanence of marriage as being a picture of Christ's permanent relationship with the church (Eph. 5:31–32).

There are clear statements claiming marriage is permanent, and remarriage after divorce is adultery. There is no clear New Testament teaching that a divorced person may remarry while their spouse is alive.

Chapter 4

Church History

THE DETERMINANT of any doctrine is neither its newness nor antiquity. Scripture is the final rule on all matters of faith and practice. Nevertheless, a historical understanding may help one think through the issues.

In the first centuries after Christ, Greek and Latin were used extensively by early Christian writers. Though not infallible, these men had a built-in understanding of Greek grammar and Roman culture that may have given them insights into the New Testament which we may not possess. They lived in the social context in which the divorce and remarriage teachings of the New Testament were expounded. We can learn something from their cultural and linguistic understanding of Scripture. In all, twenty-five out of twenty-six early church writers and two early church councils prohibited remarriage after divorce for any reason. Though their writings are not authoritative, one must take their conclusions into consideration. In an age of debate over some of the most basic doctrines, their *virtual unanimity* on divorce and remarriage is amazing. The early Christian writers who taught that remarriage after divorce for any reason was adultery include Hermas, Justin Martyr, Athenagoras, Athanasius, Theophilus of Antioch, Irenaeus, Clement of Alexandria, Origen, Tertullian, Basil of Ancyra, Basil of Caesarea, Gregory Nazianzus, Apollinaris of Laodicea, Theodore of Mopsuestia, John Chrysostom, Theodoret, Epiphanius, Ambrose, Innocent I, Pelagius, Jerome, Leo the Great, Gregory the Great, and Augustine. The Council of Elvira (AD 306) and the Council of Arles (AD 314) declare the same.

The lone patristic dissenter was a Latin bishop named Ambrosiaster. He wrote commentaries on Pauline epistles between AD 366 and 383. Little else is known about him. He is the only writer we have that allowed remarriage after divorce in limited circumstances. He allowed both partners to remarry if deserted by a pagan spouse. He did not allow remarriage if a spouse was deserted by a person who claimed to be a Christian. He allowed only the *man* to remarry in cases of adultery.

Some attempt to dismiss the consensus of the early church by claiming that these writers came to their conclusions by using only the gospels of Mark and Luke which teach only a prohibition of divorce and remarriage and do not include the "exception clause." This is not true. The gospel of Matthew was probably the most widely used book of the New Testament in the early church. Many of the early Christian writers specifically mention the Matthean "exception clause" when coming to their conclusions. Certain writers, such as Origen, Chrysostom, and Augustine specifically mention this subject in the context of commentaries on Matthew or the Sermon on the Mount.

Another attempt at dismissal is made by claiming that Jesus would have spoken to the Pharisees in Hebrew and since the early Christians writers did not know Hebrew they were confused as to the correct interpretation of the "exception clause." It is uncertain whether Jesus would have spoken to the Pharisees in Hebrew, Aramaic, or Greek. Hebrew was the scholarly language of the Jews but many Jews by this time used the Greek Septuagint translation of the Old Testament. Aramaic was the native language of Palestine but we do not know when Jesus spoke Aramaic outside of the instances recorded in the gospels. The New Testament is written in Greek and although it has been theorized that the Gospel of Matthew was first composed in Hebrew or Aramaic this is only a theory and the only manuscripts we possess are in Greek. The point being that it is uncertain what language Jesus used to speak to the Pharisees. If He did speak to them in Hebrew or Aramaic, Matthew was inspired by the Holy Spirit to record the conversation in Greek.

Although most of the early Christian writers were Gentiles they were not ignorant of Jewish divorce practices. Some of the early Christian authors also knew Hebrew. Origen compiled the *Hexapla* in which eight Hebrew and Greek versions of the Old Testament were arranged in parallel columns. Jerome was a Hebrew teacher and translated the Latin Vulgate directly from the Hebrew by-passing the Greek Septuagint. Theodoret also knew Hebrew.

Space does not permit going into detail of the writings of every early church writer. Some of the early writings are given as evidence of patristic interpretation concerning divorce and remarriage.

Probably the earliest writing we possess is from Hermas. He wrote *The Shepherd of Hermas circa* AD 160. The writings of the Shepherd are important as they were held in the highest regard by early Christians. These writings were seen as quasi-canonical and were often bound together with other portions of Scripture, specifically whatever gospels the congregation had. In his second book, *Commandments*, Hermas speaks about putting away one's wife for adultery. He writes:

> If any one has a wife who trusts in the Lord, and if he detects her in adultery, does the man sin if he continues to live with her?" And he said to me, "As long as he remains ignorant of her sin, the husband commits no transgression in living with her. But if the husband knows that his wife has gone astray, and if the woman does not repent, but persists in her fornication, and yet the husband continues to live with her, he is also guilty of her crime, and a sharer in her adultery." And I said to him, "What then, sir, is the husband to do, if his wife continues in her vicious practices? And he said, the husband should put her away, and remain by himself. But if he puts his wife away and marries another, he also commits adultery." And I said to him, "What if the woman put away should repent, and wish to return to her husband: Shall she not be taken back by her husband?" And he said to me, "Assuredly. If the husband does not take her back, he sins, and brings a great sin upon himself; for he ought to take back the sinner who has repented. But not frequently."

Hermas believed that the man who continued to live with an adulteress wife, in a sense, shared in her adultery. This was compulsory under Roman as well as Jewish law. The *Lex Iulia de adulteriis* (Roman Law of Adultery) required that a husband must send away his wife within sixty days if she was guilty of adultery. If the husband failed to do so he was guilty of *lenocinium*, a procurer or promoter of her adultery. It also was a logical application of 1 Cor. 6:15–17 which teaches that Christians should never have sexual relations with a prostitute (*pornes*).

Though allowing for divorce, Hermas saw the marriage as still intact. Because the *one flesh* bond still existed, Hermas did not allow a person to remarry after their spouse was divorced. This was his interpretation of the 'exception clause' in Matthew's Gospel. He required the husband to cease living with an adulterous wife. If the husband did not leave room for repentance and acceptance of his wife, after repentance, it was also a sin. He adds the term "but not frequently" to show that true repentance will change the actions of one's life.

Justin Martyr (AD 110–165) wrote his *First Apology circa* AD 150. Chapters 15–17 are a Christian catechism based on the Sermon on the Mount and other Gospel portions. Chapter 15 is subtitled, "What Christ Himself Taught." Justin Martyr quotes Matthew 5:32 and Matthew 19:12.

He gives no exceptions for remarriage. He lists lust and remarriage as sinning against Christ:

> Whosoever shall marry her that is divorced from another husband, commits adultery. And, there are some who have been born eunuchs of men, and some who have made themselves eunuchs for the kingdom of heaven's sake; but all cannot receive this saying. So that all who, by human law, are twice married, are in the eyes of our Master sinners, and those who look upon a woman to lust after her.

One should notice how Justin equates the eunuch saying of Matthew 19:12 with the subject of abstaining from a second remarriage after divorce.

Justin also shows that he believed Christians should separate from an adulterous spouse but that does not give them the right to remarry. *Second Apology*, chapter 2 reads:

> But when her husband had gone into Alexandria, and was reported to be conducting himself worse than ever, she—that she might not, by continuing in matrimonial connection with him, and by sharing his table and his bed, become a partaker also in wickedness and impieties—gave him what you call a bill of divorce, and was separated from him.

Athenagoras wrote his *Plea for Christians* around AD 177:

> For we bestow our attention, not on the study of words, but on the exhibition and teaching of actions, that a person should either remain as he was born, or be content with one marriage; for a second marriage is only a specious adultery. For whosoever puts away his wife, says He and marries another, commits adultery; not permitting a man to send her away whose virginity he has brought to an end, nor to marry again. For he who deprives himself of his first wife, even though she be dead, is a cloaked adulterer, resisting the hand of God, because in the beginning God made one man and one woman, and dissolving the strictest union of flesh with flesh, formed for the intercourse of the race.

Athenagoras was writing this letter to the Emperors Marcus Aurelius Anoninus and Lucius Aurelius Commodus. The purpose of it was to defend the rationality of the Christian faith and the superiority of its morals. Athenagoras uses marriage as one example of Christianity's higher standards. Pagans divorce their wives and marry again, Christians do not. Athenagoras' interpretation of Matthew 19 is that a second marriage equals adultery. He appears to be influenced by Phrygian Montanism for not allowing remarriage after either spouse's death. This does not nullify the fact that he saw divorce and remarriage to be a form of adultery.

Clement of Alexandria (ca. AD 153–217) was the headmaster of the Christian school in Alexandria, Egypt from AD 190–202. Book II of the *Stromata* or *Miscellanies* was written to show that Christian morality was superior to paganism. Book III is an exposition on Christian marriage.

Clement has this to say regarding the biblical understanding of marriage:

> Now that the Scripture counsels marriage, and allows no release from the union, is expressly contained in the law, "Thou shall not put away thy wife, except for the cause of fornication;" and it regards as fornication, the marriage of those separated while the other is alive . . . "He that takes a woman that has been put away," it is said, "commits adultery; and if one puts away his wife, he makes her an adulteress," that is compels her to commit adultery. And not only is he who puts her away guilty of this, but he who takes her, by giving to the woman the opportunity of sinning; for did he not take her, she would return to her husband.

Clement appears to quote Matthew 5:32 and 19:9. He sees the exception clause as allowing only separation or divorce. It does not allow for remarriage. A complete reading of Clement's works tells us the purpose for the divorce is to allow the believer to separate from that which is unclean, namely a fornicating spouse. If the spouse repents of their sin, they become clean and are to be received back unto conjugal relations. The reason for divorce is not to permit remarriage. He claims remarriage after divorce is adultery in every instance while the other spouse lives.

Theophilus (AD 115–181 or 188). Little is known about Theophilus. It appears that he was born into a pagan household but came to Christ through reading the Scriptures. Eusebius writes that he was sixth in succession of elders following Barnabas in Antioch in Syria. These were Eros, Cornelius, Hero, Ignatius, and Euodius. Theophilus became an elder in Antioch the eighth year of the reign of Marcus Aurelius, AD 168. The works of Theophilus were written as an apologetic to his friend Autolycus an idolater and scorner of Christians.

In book 3, chapter 13 Theophilus writes:

> And the voice of the Gospel teaches still more concerning chastity, saying: "Whosoever looks on a woman who is not his own wife, to lust after her has committed adultery already with her in his

heart." "And he that marries," say the Gospel, "her that is divorced from her husband, commits adultery; and whosoever puts away his wife, except for the cause of fornication, causes her to commit adultery."

Theophilus uses these verses from Matthew 5 in relation to Proverbs 6:27–29. It appears that he believed that remarriage after divorce was to be equated with being burned with fire and the man that remarries, "goes into a married woman shall not be innocent."

Irenaeus (AD 120–202) was born in Asia Minor and raised in Smyrna. He claims to have known Polycarp who was taught by the apostle John. In *Against Heresies* Irenaeus quotes Genesis 2:24 and Matthew 19:7–8 to show God's original intent for the permanence of marriage. He shows that the Mosaic Law was enacted only because of the hardness of men's hearts:

> And not only so, but the Lord also showed that certain precepts were enacted for them by Moses, on account of their hardness of heart, and because of their unwillingness to be obedient, when, on their saying to Him, "Why then did Moses command to give a writing of divorcement, and to send away a wife?" He said to them, "Because of the hardness of their hearts he permitted these things to you; but from the beginning it was not so"; thus exculpating Moses as a faithful servant, but acknowledging one God, who from the beginning made male and female, and reproving them as hard hearted and disobedient.

Tertullain (AD 145–220) was an elder in Carthage. He wrote in Latin and was a voluminous theologian. He was born into a pagan household and seems to have been educated in Rome. Tertullian transitions from an orthodox Christian period to semi-Montantist and Montanist periods. His Montanist beliefs led him astray in certain areas. Nevertheless, his writings concerning the permanence of marriage reflect the general consensus of the early church. In *Against Marcion* book 4 chapter 24 Tertullian's writings are quite lengthy. The reader is encouraged to obtain a copy and read it in context. Chapter 24 includes these statements:

> But Christ prohibits divorce, saying, "whosoever puts away his wife and marries another, commits adultery; and whosoever marries her that is put away from her husband also commits adultery." In order to forbid divorce, he makes it unlawful to marry a woman that has been put away . . . For in the Gospel of Matthew he says, "whosoever shall put away his wife, except for the cause of fornication, causes her to commit adultery." He also is deemed equally guilty of adultery, who marries a woman put away by her husband.

Origen (AD 185–254) wrote extensive commentaries on the Scriptures. He writes this in his *Commentary on Matthew*:

> But as a woman is an adulteress, even though she seems to be married to a man, while the former husband is still living, so also the man who seems to marry her who has been put away, does not so much marry her as commit adultery with her according to the declaration of our Savior.

The Council of Arles (AD 314) *Canon* 10 states:

> As regards those who find their wives to be guilty of adultery, and who being Christians are, though young men, forbidden to marry, we decree that, so far as may be, counsel be given them not to take other wives, while their own, though guilty of adultery, are yet living.

Basil of Caesarea (AD 329–379) is also known as Basil "The Great." His brother was Gregory of Nyssa and Gregory Nazianzus was his good friend. He was born into a wealthy Christian family in Cappadocia. He was trained in rhetoric at Constantinople and Athens. He left this to devote himself to a simple life of scholarship. With his friend Gregory Nazianzus he compiled the works of Origen. In one of his numerous letters Basil writes:

> The woman who has been abandoned by her husband, ought, in my judgment, to remain as she is. The Lord said "If anyone leaves his wife, saving for the cause of fornication, he causes her to commit adultery;" thus by calling her an adulteress, He excludes her from intercourse with another man. For how can the man being guilty, having caused adultery, and the woman, go without blame, when she is called an adulteress by the Lord for having intercourse with another man?

Gregory Nazianzus (ca. AD 325–391) is also known as "The Theologian." He was a friend of Basil the Great and a defender of the doctrine of the Trinity. Contrary to modern interpreters who claim that the early Christian writers were deficient in their knowledge of Jewish Law Gregory writes:

> Now the Law grants divorce for every cause; but Christ not for every cause; but He allows only separation from the whore; and in all other things commands patience. He allows to put away the fornicatress, because she corrupts the offspring; but in all other matters let us be patient, as many as have receive the yoke of matrimony.

Jerome (ca. AD 347–407) was a native of Venetia and was baptized in AD 360. For several years after that he was a wandering student in Rome and Gaul. In AD 386 Jerome went to Palestine, and there through the financial assistance of Paula, a wealthy Roman lady whom he had taught Hebrew, he lived in a monastic retreat at Bethlehem. He led this retreat for thirty five years. Jerome is most famous for his Latin translation of the Bible, *Biblia Sacra Vulgata*. Being an accomplished teacher of Hebrew he went beyond the use of the Greek Septuagint in translating the Old Testament. This is important to note as modern defenders of the Erasmian interpretation often claim that since some of the early Christian writers did not know Hebrew they were led astray in their interpretation of the Lord's teaching on divorce and remarriage.

In AD 394 Jerome wrote *a letter to Amandus* in which he included a reply to a question posed to him by a sister regarding whether a woman who is divorced because of sexual sins by her husband can fellowship with the saints without first repenting. Jerome writes:

> I find joined to your letter of inquiries a short paper containing the following words: "ask him, whether a woman who has left her husband on the grounds that he is an adulterer and sodomite and has found herself compelled to take another may in the lifetime of him whom she first left be in communion with the church without repenting for her fault." As I read the case put I recall the verse "they make excuses for their sins." We are all human and all indulgent to our own faults; and what our own will leads us to do we attribute to the necessity of nature. It is as though a young man were to say, "I am overcome by my body, the glow of nature kindles my passions, the structure of my frame and its reproductive organs call for sexual intercourse." Or again a murderer might say, "I was in want, I stood in need of food, I had nothing to cover me. If I shed the blood of another, it was to save myself from dying of cold and hunger."
>
> Tell the sister, therefore, who thus enquires of me concerning her condition, not my sentence but that of the apostle. "Know ye not, brethren (for I speak to them that know the law), how that the law has dominion over a man as long as he lives? For the woman who has a husband is bound by the law to her husband as long as he lives; but if her husband is dead; she is loosed from the law of her husband. So then if while her husband lives, she is married to another, she will be called an adulterer" . . . The apostle has thus cut away every plea and has clearly declared that, if a woman marries again while her husband is living, she is an adulteress . . . A husband may be an adulterer or a sodomite, he may be stained

with every crime and may have been left by his wife because of his sins; yet he is still her husband and, so long as he lives, she may not marry another.

The apostle does not promulgate this decree on his own authority but on that of Christ who speaks in him. For he has followed the words of Christ in the gospel: "whosoever shall put away his wife, saving for the cause of fornication, causes her to commit adultery: and whosoever shall marry her that is divorce commits adultery." Mark what he says: "whosoever shall marry her that is divorced commits adultery." Whether she has put away her husband or her husband her, the man who marries her is still an adulterer.

Therefore if your sister, who, as she says, has been forced into a second union, wishes to receive the body of Christ and not be counted an adulteress, let her repent; so far at least from the time she begins to repent to have no further intercourse with that second husband who ought to be called not a husband but an adulterer.

John Chrysostom (ca. AD 347–407) lived a pure and simple life. He was called "Chrysostom" (golden mouthed) shortly after his death for his skill as an expositor and orator. In his *Homilies on the Gospel of Matthew* he has this to say regarding the passages which include the "exception clause":

And observe Him everywhere addressing His discourse to the man. Thus, "He that puts away his wife," says He, "causes her to commit adultery, and he that marries a woman put away, commits adultery." That is, the former, though he take not another wife, by that act alone hath made himself liable to blame, having made the first an adulteress; the later again is become an adulterer by taking her who is another's. For tell me not this, "the other hath cast her out;" nay, for when cast out she continued to be the wife of him that expelled her . . . And not thus only, but in another way also He hath lightened the enactment: forasmuch as even for him He leaves one manner of dismissal, when He says, "Except for the cause of fornication"; since the matter had else come round again to the same issue. For if He had commanded to keep her in the house, though defiling herself with many, He would have made the matter end again in adultery.

But mark Him arguing strongly not from the creation only, but also from His command. For He said not, that He made one man and one woman only, but that He also gave this command that the one man should be joined to the one woman. But if it had been His will that he should put this one away, and bring in another, when He had made one man, He would have formed many women. But now both by the manner of the creation, and by the manner of law giving, He showed that one man must dwell with one woman continually, and never break off from her.

Chrysostom saw the marriage as remaining intact even if a wife is divorced or expelled from the home. He allows the man to separate from a fornicating wife so that he is not defiled by his wife's adultery. He does not allow either the man or the woman to remarry in such instances.

Augustine (AD 354–430) was one of the most prolific writers in the history of the church. Augustine taught marriage was a divine mystery and an analogy of the unity of the church. He wrote nine Moral Treatises. *On the Good of Marriage* reads:

"For whosoever puts away his wife, except for the case of fornication, makes her to commit adultery." To such a degree is that marriage compact entered upon a matter of a certain sacrament, that it is not void even by separation itself, since, so long as her husband lives, even by whom she hath been left, she commits adultery, in case she be married to another: and he who hath left her, is the cause of this evil. But I marvel, if, as it is allowed to put away a wife who is an adulteress, so it be allowed, having put her away, to marry another. For holy Scripture causes a hard knot in this matter, in that the Apostle says, that, by commandment of the Lord, the wife ought not to depart from her husband, but, in case she shall have departed, to remain unmarried, or to be reconciled to her husband; whereas surely she ought not to depart and remain unmarried, save from an husband that is an adulterer, lest by withdrawing from him, who is not an adulterer, she cause him to commit adultery. But I see not how the man can have permission to marry another, in case he have left an adulteress, when a woman has not to be married to another, in case she have left an adulterer. And, this being the case, so strong is that bond of fellowship in married persons, that, although it is tied for the sake of begetting children, not even for the sake of begetting children is it loosed. For it is in a man's power to put away a wife that is barren, and marry one of whom to have children. And yet it is not allowed; and now indeed, in our times, and after the usage of Rome, neither to marry in addition, so as to have more than one wife living: and surely, in case of an adulteress or adulterer being left, it would be possible that more men should be born, if either the woman were married to another, or the man should marry another. And yet, if to prescribe, who is there but it must make him attentive to learn what is the meaning of this so great strength of the marriage bond? . . . Seeing that the compact of marriage is not done away by divorce intervening; so that they continue wedded persons one to another, even after separation; and commit adultery with those, with whom they shall be joined, even after their own divorce, either the woman with a man, or the man with a woman.

On Marriage and Concupiscence states:

So enduring, indeed, are the rights of marriage between those who have contracted them, as long as they both live, that even they are looked on as man and wife still, who have separated from one another, rather than they between a new connection has been formed. For by this new connection they would not be guilty of adultery, if the previous matrimonial relation did not still continue. If the husband dies, with whom a true marriage was made, a true marriage is now possible by a connection which would before have been adultery. Thus between the conjugal pair, as long as they live, the nuptial bond has a permanent obligation, and can be canceled neither by separation nor by union with another.

Augustine begins his argument by citing Matthew 5:32. This passage contains the "exception clause" which allows divorce when fornication has been committed. He calls marriage a sacrament but uses the word in a different sense than later Roman Catholicism. Marriage is such a "compact" that separation does not allow the woman to remarry if her husband deserts her. If the woman remarries she commits adultery. The deserting husband is said to be the cause of this evil. Augustine marvels that society allows a man to remarry after putting away an adulterous wife. He recognizes this "causes a hard knot" but realizes that Paul's command in I Corinthians 7:10–11 says the woman is not to depart. If she does depart she is to remain unmarried. Augustine synthesizes these passages by allowing the woman to depart only in the case of an adulterous husband. He does not allow the woman to remarry. Since Scripture forbids the woman to remarry after departing from an adulterous husband Augustine does not see how a man could have permission to remarry after leaving an adulterous wife. Men and women are married for the purpose of procreation, this purpose cannot loose them. Scripture forbids remarriage after divorce even in cases of adultery. If they remarry after divorce they commit adultery with whom they are joined.

Leo the Great (ca. AD 390–461) was born in Tuscany. He became the bishop of Rome in AD 440. He wrote *a letter to Nicaetas*, bishop of Aquileia, regarding women who had remarried when their soldier husbands had been taken prisoner. He believed that the original marriage bond still existed and the women who remarried should return to their original husbands. Those who refused to return to their first husband were not permitted fellowship. Leo writes:

> But because we know it is written that "a woman is joined to a man by God," and again, we are aware of the precept that "what God hath joined, man may not put asunder," we are bound to hold that the compact of the lawful marriage must be renewed . . . And if any women are so possessed by love of their later husbands as to prefer to remain with them than to return to their lawful partners, they are deservedly to be branded: so that they be even deprived of the church's communion.

Gregory I is also known as Gregory "The Great." He became the bishop of Rome in AD 590. His rule finalized the division between the Eastern and Western institutional church. His ascension to power also marks the unofficial demarcation between early and medieval church history. In a letter to Adrian Gregory writes:

> For although mundane law declares that marriage may be dissolved for the sake of conversion against the will of either party, yet divine law does not permit this to be done. For, save for the cause of fornication, a man is on no account allowed to put away his wife, seeing that after the husband and wife have been made one body by the copulation of wedlock, it cannot be in part converted, and in part remain in the world.

Although the final determinant of any doctrine is Scripture, one must take these writings into consideration. If Jesus did allow remarriage after divorce, why do we have no record of it being taught or practiced? Where did the no remarriage doctrine come from?

Modern detractors claim that the early Christians did not understand Hebrew or use the Gospel of Matthew to come to their interpretive conclusions. The fact is that some of them did know Hebrew and most of them directly quote the Matthean Gospel text. Some of them interact with Jewish laws and traditions and show how the teachings of Christ regarding divorce and remarriage are superior. It cannot be that they simply did not understand the Old Testament. Most of them read Greek copies of the Old Testament and some of them read the Hebrew. Some of them mention Jewish divorce and remarriage practices.

The early Christian writers had a first hand linguistic and cultural understanding of the teachings of Jesus and Paul in the New Testament. Many of them spoke and wrote Greek as a primary or secondary language.

Although separated by centuries and various geographic and cultural boundaries they had a virtual consensus in their understanding of the permanence of marriage. This consensus does not appear to come from reading one another's writings but from reading the New Testament. Their view was the majority view of the church in the East until the 6th century and of the church in the West until the 16th century.

In the 13th century Aquinas taught that marriage was a "sacrament" that conveys divine grace to the recipients. The Roman Catholic Church adopted this view and further erred by allowing divorce and remarriage in the form of ecclesiastical annulments. These views were canonized by the Council of Trent in the 16th century.

In 1519 the Catholic-humanist Erasmus stated that the innocent spouse in matters of adultery and desertion had the right to remarry. Though the idea did not originate with him it can be shown that under his influence this view gained broad acceptance. In Erasmus' day salvation was said to come only through the institutional Roman Catholic Church. Erasmus saw injurious and unhappy marriages. He believed that church courts could be established to grant people divorces for serious reasons. The innocent party would then be granted permission to remarry by ecclesiastical authorities. Erasmus was aware of the scriptural teaching of no remarriage after divorce. He was a Greek scholar, yet his views were more influenced by social concerns than careful exegesis of relevant texts.

Since Erasmus allowed people to see their spouse as figuratively dead it is admitted that many today do not strictly follow his exegesis but only his conclusions. Most Christians today do not know this interpretation follows the tradition of Erasmus. The term "Erasmian" will be used to refer to those who allow remarriage after divorce because of adultery or desertion. It is not a derogatory term but one of convenience.

Martin Luther (1483–1546) sought reform of indulgences in the Roman Catholic Church. When Luther broke from the Church, Erasmus opposed this move. Nevertheless, Erasmus' ideas were latched onto by the Reformers. Luther believed that the innocent party of an adulterous situation could divorce and remarry. He taught that since the Old Testament legislated the death penalty for adultery, the adulterous spouse should be looked upon as figuratively dead. This type of legal fiction now allowed the 'innocent' spouse the right to remarry. Luther also allowed divorce and remarriage for impotence, refusal of conjugal rights, desertion, and ignorance of a previously contracted marriage. Perhaps his true views can be seen in how he actually applied the doctrine. Philip of Hesse was a supporter of Martin Luther. In 1540 Philip married Margaret Von Der Saale.

Philip of Hesse was already married and had not even legally divorced his first wife. Luther did not confront this situation but simply urged the matter be kept secret.

John Calvin (1509–1564) took a more conservative approach to divorce and remarriage while still retaining some liberal conclusions. He rightly understood Deuteronomy 24:1–4 to only be a restraint upon a second remarriage. He did not see this passage as teaching approval of divorce and remarriage by God. Calvin did resort to legal fiction in allowing the innocent partner in the case of adultery to consider his or her spouse figuratively dead. He allowed the deserted partner to remarry by way of assumption that the deserter would enter into another conjugal relationship.

In 1643 John Milton taught that Christ did not condemn divorce and remarriage, but only the injury they caused. He believed a couple could divorce for almost any reason, including mutual consent. He was thought of as radical and heretical for this view. His view comes closest to what is practiced by some Evangelicals today.

In 1648 the views of the Reformers were canonized into Protestant law in the Westminster Confession. One man who influenced the acceptance of divorce and remarriage in the Westminster Confession was most likely John Lightfoot, author of *A Commentary on the New Testament from the Talmud and Hebraica*. He mistakenly believed that "some indecency" in Deuteronomy 24:1 referred to adultery. This led him to the erroneous conclusion that *porneia* in the Matthean exception clause was a reference to adultery as justification for divorce and remarriage.

The Westminster Confession in chapter 24 states:

> *Section V* - Adultery or fornication committed after a contract, being detected before marriage, giveth just occasion to the innocent party to dissolve that contract [Matt. 1:18–20]. In the case of adultery after marriage, it is lawful for the innocent party to sue out a divorce [Matt. 5:32], and after the divorce to marry another, *as if the offending party were dead* [Matt. 19:9; Rom. 7:2–3. *italics mine*].

> *Section VI* - Although the corruption of man be such as is apt to study arguments, unduly to put asunder those whom God hath joined together in marriage; yet nothing but adultery, or such willful desertion as can no way be remedied by the Church or civil magistrate, is cause sufficient of dissolving the bond of marriage [Matt. 19:8–9; 1 Cor. 7:15; Matt. 19:6]; where in a public and orderly course of proceeding is to be observed, and the persons

concerned in it not left to their own wills and discretion in their own case [Deut. 24:1–4].

Although the leaders of the Reformation sought to allow divorce and remarriage for cases of adultery and desertion the acceptance of such teaching was limited. Even among Lutherans and Presbyterians divorce and remarriage was not widely practiced. The Anglican Church and some eastern Christian groups held firm and refused to accept the practice of divorce and remarriage. Many Anabaptist groups rejected the Erasmian interpretation altogether. In practice it was not until the 1960's that western evangelical Christians began accepting divorce and remarriage in a broad measure. In the 1960's and 1970's numerous evangelical doctrinal statements began to change to allow for remarriage after divorce. In the last fifty years the evangelical church has become greatly influenced by secular culture and accepted the widespread practice of divorce and remarriage for almost any reason. In many Eastern churches the practice of allowing divorce and remarriage comes mainly from the influence of missionaries from the West. In the western Evangelical church the current majority position is that a person may divorce and remarry once but any subsequent divorces are considered suspect. This shows the weakness of the position. If divorce and remarriage is allowed (sometimes encouraged) it should not matter how many marriages a person contracts. The Scriptures teach that a person may abstain from marriage or have one marriage during the life of their spouse. Anything beyond this is considered adultery.

Summary

The early Christian writers had a virtual consensus in saying that remarriage after divorce, for any reason, was adultery. The western Church held to a no remarriage view until the 16th century. At this point Erasmus taught a divorced person may remarry, not by exegesis of the "exception clause" but by interpretive legal fiction based on Old Testament law. The Reformers latched onto this view and canonized it in the Westminster Confession. It has held sway over much of the Protestant Church ever since.

The Reformation was an attempt to return the church to first century beliefs and practices. The Reformers held the early Christian writers in high esteem. Calvin in his opening address to Francis, the King of France, stated:

So far are we from despising them, that if this were the proper place, it would give us no trouble to support the greater part of the doctrines which we now hold are their suffrages.[1]

In some ways the Reformers returned to the faith and practices of the first century church. Concerning the issue of divorce and remarriage the evidence shows the Reformers failed. Tony Lane, a lecturer at London Bible College, shows how a historical understanding may help one to think through the issues:

> If Jesus did allow remarriage, presumably it happened. How did it cease to happen, despite the fact that this teaching was known, leaving no trace either of a period when it happened or any controversy. Such a theory is no more plausible than a theory that the "Lord's day" was originally on a Friday and that it changed to Sunday without leaving any trace of the change and without any controversy over the change.[2]

Those who allow for remarriage after divorce should remember two things. First, the Reformers allowed for remarriage based upon interpretive legal fiction. Few seem to be willing to do this today. Second, the arguments presented today concerning the 'exception clause' are recent and were not used by early Christian writers or the Reformers.

Modern day Erasmian interpreters believe that the early church was out of touch with the teachings of Jesus regarding divorce and remarriage. They claim that the early Christians were unduly influenced by asceticism which led them to incorrect conclusions regarding the permanence of marriage. It is more probable that both those who practice and those who justify divorce and remarriage in the modern evangelical church have come to incorrect conclusions regarding the permanence of marriage because they are unduly influenced by modern culture.

---

1. John Calvin, *Institutes of the Christian Religion*, p. 10.
2. Tony Lane, *May a Divorced Person Remarry*, p. 4.

Chapter 5

Permanence of Adultery

THE PURPOSE of this chapter is to determine whether remarriage after divorce constitutes a continuous state of adultery or a one time act with no continuing repercussions. Although many in the church teach that remarriage after divorce should not be considered adultery, it is not the opinion of the majority that will count on judgment day. It is only God's word and pleasing the Lord that matters.

Adultery

The Bible clearly states that those who remarry after divorce "commit adultery." The biblical evidence is as follows:

Matthew 5:32b ". . . causes her to commit *adultery* (*moichasthai*); and whoever marries a divorced woman commits *adultery* (*moichatai*)."

Matthew 19:9b ". . . and marries another, commits *adultery* (*moichatai*); and whoever marries her who is divorced commits *adultery* (*moichatai*)."

Mark 10:11–12 "Whoever divorces his wife and marries another commits *adultery* (*moichatai*) against her; and if a wife herself divorces her husband and marries another she commits *adultery* (*mochatai*)."

Luke 16:18 "Every one who divorces his wife and marries another commits *adultery* (*moicheuei*); and whoever marries her who is divorced from her husband commits *adultery* (*moicheuei*)."

Romans 7:3 "So then if, while her husband lives, she marries another man, she will be called an *adulteress* (*moichalis*); but if her husband dies she is free from that law, so that she is no *adulteress* (*moichalida*), though she has married another man."

Although Matthew's Gospel gives one exception for divorce, *fornication* (*porneia*), it can be shown that this exception clause allows only for divorce in limited instances and the divorce does not include the right to remarry. In both passages of Matthew's Gospel it is claimed that the person who remarries still commits adultery. Ten times the New Testament calls remarriage after divorce adultery. This is where our study will begin.

The Verb Tense

One of the main considerations regarding the permanence of adultery is the use of the *verb tense* when Jesus pronounces that those who divorce and remarry commit adultery. Most often it is the *present tense* that controls the meaning of adultery in these sentences.

Matthew 5:32 uses the present active indicative (*poiei*) "makes her" in conjunction with the present infinitive (*moichasthai*) "to commit adultery." This is the reading of the majority text. The modern eclectic text uses the aorist infinitive (*moicheuthenai*). It then reads that whoever marries a divorced woman commits adultery (*moichatai*), present middle/passive indicative. The middle/passive form can literally be translated "cause oneself to commit adultery" or "be an adulterer."

Matthew 19:9 twice uses the present middle/passive indicative (*moichatai*) "to be an adulterer."

Mark 10:11–12 twice uses the present middle/passive indicative (*moichatai*) "to be an adulterer."

Luke 16:18 twice uses the present active indicative (*moicheuei*) "commits adultery."

Romans 7:3 uses nouns for the word "adulteress." The main verb that modifies this is a future active indicative (*chrematisei*) "she will be called." The other modifying verb form is the present active infinitive (*einai*) "to be."

The purpose of this section is to give the reader a basic understanding of the present tense as it relates to "kind of action" as well as "time of action." This will be important as we discuss the use of the verb tense as it relates to the phrase "commits adultery." The following paragraphs on the *Present Tense* are a summary from the works of Dana and Mantey—*A Manual Grammar of the Greek New Testament*; Robertson—*Grammar of the Greek New Testament*; Blass, DeBrunner, and Funk—*A Greek Grammar of the New Testament and Other Early Christian Literature*.

One important element of tense in Greek is kind of action or progress. Time of action is secondary in most cases. The action may be viewed as continuous, complete, or simply occurring without reference to progress. The three fundamental tenses in Greek are: *present*, representing continuous action; *perfect*, representing completed action; and *aorist*, representing undefined action. The basic meaning of aorist (*aoristos*) is "undefined" or "without limits." Continuous action is primarily represented by the present tense and this is primarily with reference to present time. Continuous action in the past is represented by the imperfect, and continuous action in the future is represented by the future tense (Dana and Mantey, p. 178; Robertson, p. 824).

The fundamental meaning of the present tense is that of progress. It is at its root a linear tense. Although this is the main significance of the present tense it is not the only meaning. When the indicative mood is used with present tense the element of time is more relevant. In dealing with the present tense one must consider not only the fundamental force of the tense, but also the meaning of the verb root, and the significance of the context (Dana and Mantey, p. 181).

The present tense may be used to express an action simply (punctiliar), a process (durative or linear), or a state (perfective or perfect) (Robertson, p. 865, 869). Although the present tense may be used in an aoristic sense the present tense more frequently denotes durative or linear action (Robertson, p. 879).

The present tense may be further broken down into "regular" and "special" meanings (Dana and Mantey, p. 182). The most basic (regular) meaning of the present tense is that of the progressive present. This is nearest the root idea of the tense. It shows action as a durative progress or state of persistence. The point of view can be descriptive, retroactive, or used to denote the continuation of existing results. The present tense can also be seen as customary. This is used to denote that which habitually occurs, or may be reasonably expected to occur. The temporal element is remote since the act is assumed to be true in the past or future, as well as the present (Dana and Mantey, p 184). The regular use of the present tense can also be iterative, that which occurs repeatedly at successive intervals (Dana and Mantey, p. 185; Blass, Debruner, and Funk, p. 166).

Special uses of the present tense include: Aoristic, Futuristic, Historical, Tendential, and Static. It is improbable that the present tense used by Jesus, "commits adultery (*moichatai*)," should be considered Futuristic, Historical, Tendential, or Static therefore these will not be dealt with at this time. General truths may be expressed by the aoristic present. Much of the time the aoristic present is used where a punctiliar act takes place at the moment of speaking (Blass, Debruner, and Funk, p. 167).

One sub-group of the aoristic present is the gnomic present. The difference between the gnomic aorist and the gnomic present is that the present may be durative (Robertson, p. 836). Some claim that the statement "commits adultery (*moichaai*)" is a gnomic present.

The reader should not become confused at this point. There is a *present* Greek tense and an *aorist* Greek tense. They are separate forms and tenses. This being said it must be noted that the present tense can be translated like an aorist in certain contexts. The basic idea of the aorist is it is "undefined" or "unlimited." It is punctiliar (momentary), not linear. It represents the action as occurring or having occurred without reference to time. Blass, Debrunner, and Funk claim that the action is conceived as a point with either the beginning or the end emphasized, or the action may be conceived as a whole irrespective of its duration (p. 166). The aorist tense is neither past, nor present, nor future with reference to time. It relates to "kind" of action (*aktionsarten*) rather than "time" of action. It is not, as commonly, but erroneously defined, a "once for all" event.

Durative or Aoristic

With the ground work laid for basic uses of the present tense it must now be decided how the words "commit adultery" (*moichatai*) should be understood in relation to the subject of divorce and remarriage. No matter what view one takes of the "exception clause" of Matthew 19:9 the question must be answered. Even those who allow remarriage after divorce in cases of adultery will have to wrestle with this issue. Of the divorces that occur in the evangelical church many occur for a multitude of reasons where adultery plays no part. Jesus boldly proclaimed that remarriage after such a divorce constitutes adultery.

Eight times the gospels use the *present tense* to state that those who remarry after divorce "commit adultery." Romans 7:3 further uses the *future indicative* once and a *present infinitive* once. It is claimed that if the present tense in the gospels is understood as durative or progressive then the remarried person is committing continual or repeated acts of adultery. It is then claimed that if the present tense is to be understood as aoristic or gnomic then the divorcee does not continue to commit adultery after a subsequent remarriage. It is not that simple even if the present tense "commits adultery" (*moichatai*) is aoristic or gnomic, the effects of adultery may still apply to those who continue in a sexual relationship.

Grammar and syntax regulate the formation and usage of words in a sentence. The grammatical rules are derived *from* analyzing the various uses of a word in context. They are determined by *how* the word is used. The grammatical usage is governed internally by the text itself. There are no external sources that state *how* the word "commits adultery" (*moichatai*) should be understood. The understanding of the word comes from how the word is used in context. Even if every other use of the present tense in Matthew's Gospel was aoristic that does not mean that "commits adultery" (*moichatai*) in Matthew 5:32 and 19:9 should be taken that way. The converse is also true. The present may predominantly be a progressive or durative tense but this does not necessarily mean that Jesus uses it this way when He states "commits adultery" (*moichatai*).

It is possible that "commits adultery" (*moichatai*) should be taken in an aoristic or gnomic sense. It is also possible that the present tense "commits adultery" (*moichatai*) should be taken as durative or progressive. There is certainly nothing that would prohibit it from being understood as durative or progressive. It is the word interpreted in context that determines the *type* of present tense used not some external definition applied to the text.

Aoristic or Gnomic Implications

If the present tense "commits adultery" (*moichatai*) is to be taken as progressive or durative it would mean that the remarried person continually commits adultery each and every time they have sexual relations after the remarriage. The opposite is not necessarily true if the present tense is to be taken as aoristic or gnomic.

The aoristic (punctiliar) present sets forth the event as now occurring (Dana and Mantey, p. 184). Just because it is now occurring does not mean that there are no residual effects in the future. Dana and Mantey list Acts 9:34 as an example of the aoristic present: *"Aeneas, Jesus Christ heals (hiatai) you."* In this example the healing is stated as presently occurring but there will be lasting effects for a period of time in the future. The present may combine both aoristic action with continuous or durative results (Robertson, p. 865).

The gnomic present is actually a sub-group under the aoristic (punctiliar) present (Robertson, p. 866). The gnomic present expresses general truth but this does not mean there are no continuing consequences. The gnomic present is timeless in reality, meaning that it is true of all time (Robertson, p. 836, 864). It is sometimes called the proverbial present because this use of the present occurs in proverbial statements or general maxims about that which occurs at all times. Robertson lists First Corinthians 15:42 as an example of a gnomic present: "The body it is sown (*speiretai*) in corruption, it is raised (*egeiretai*) in incorruption." Certainly these two gnomic presents have lasting implications in the future.

85

Another possible option for the present tense "commits adultery" (*moichatai*) is the iterative present. The iterative present represents an action that is repeated each time. When applied to "commits adultery (*moichatai*) it would mean that each time a remarried couple had sexual relations they would be committing a further act of adultery.

Romans 7:3

In Romans 7:3 the future active indicative "she will be called" (*chrematisei*) is used with reference to the description, adulteress, applied to the woman who remarries. The future almost always carries with it an element of time (Robertson, p. 876; Dana and Mantey, p. 191). Instead of mainly representing progress, as do the present and the prefect tenses, the general perspective is aoristic or punctiliar. The context will sometimes require the future tense to be interpreted as progressive but most of the time this is not the case. Romans 7:3 is most likely an example of a gnomic future which means that it is an act that is true of all time (Robertson, p.876).

Romans 7:3 also uses the present infinitive "to be" (*einai*). Technically infinitives are verbal nouns and not just a mood (Dana and Mantey, p. 208). They are substantival in nature and can occupy the ground of both a verb and a noun. Paul uses the infinitive as a substantive to show that if the woman's husband dies she is not an adulteress if she remarries. The implication when taken in context with the first part of Romans 7:3 is that she is an adulteress if she marries another man while her first husband is still alive.

Conclusion

The present tense statement of Jesus "commits adultery" is most likely gnomic in meaning. This being said there is no conclusive evidence as to whether the present tense "commits adultery" (*moichatai*)" should be taken as linear (durative or progressive) or punctiliar (aoristic or gnomic). If it is linear then continual adultery would be implied; since this is a primary meaning of the tense this may be what Jesus was speaking of. If the present tense is punctiliar this in no way means the remarriage is not continuous adultery. The aoristic present expresses an action (*aktionsarten*) as taking place. It is basically timeless. Every act of adultery including sexual relations after remarriage takes place at a specific point in time. Classifying the present indicative as aoristic or gnomic does not rule out the existence of future effects or continuing results from the act of adultery. The use of the present tense does not indicate that continuous or repeated acts of adultery do not occur after remarriage.

A Logically and Biblically Consistent View

A correct understanding of the present tense is not the only deciding factor in determining whether those who remarry after divorce continue in a permanent state of adultery. Logic used in conjunction with a biblical view of the one flesh bond and sin must also be taken into consideration.

A common view is that if one's spouse commits adultery they are free to obtain a legal divorce and then remarry. There are numerous biblical and logical problems with this view. The Bible teaches that the one flesh bond is severed only by death. The person who has an unfaithful spouse is to forgive them not divorce them. Jesus commanded His followers to forgive others who sin against them seventy times seven. How much more should a husband who is commanded to love his wife as Christ loved the church forgive his own flesh? (See Eph. 5:25, 29.)

The reason that remarriage after divorce is considered adultery is because of the nature of the one flesh bond. When a person remarries they enter into a sexual relationship with another person outside of the original God ordained marriage. Mankind was created to be in a monogamous sexual relationship. Anything outside of this is considered sin. The claim is sometimes made that remarriage after divorce is an act of adultery but not continual or persistent adultery. Jesus claimed that it is the remarriage of a divorced person that is the cause of their adultery (Matt. 5:32; 19:9; Mark 10:11–12; Luke 16:18). The idea being that after the remarriage ceremony both parties will enter into another sexual relationship.

When a person enters into a sexual relationship outside of the original one flesh bond it is considered adultery. It is not the second wedding ceremony that makes them an adulterer it is the sexual relations committed after the ceremony that makes them an adulterer. This is because divorce does not make one single again. A legal divorce does not end a person's one flesh bond from their first marriage. If divorce severed or dissolved the one flesh bond then adultery could not occur in remarriage. Adultery occurs in remarriage because the legally divorced spouse is still married to their first marriage partner. Divorced persons who remarry may be recognized by the state as being legally married but "from the beginning it was not so." A legal document called *divorce* by the state, from God's point of view, does not break the marriage bond, else remarriage would not be called adultery.

If the sexual relations entered into after a second marriage ceremony are considered to be an act of adultery then every subsequent sexual act in that relationship would also be considered adultery. To believe that the first sexual act is adultery while subsequent acts are not is illogical. If sexual relations at the beginning of a second marriage are considered adultery they would continue to be considered as such upon each encounter. The reason is that the one flesh bond from the first marriage continues to exist.

Some claim that the second marriage and one act of subsequent sexual relations breaks the first one flesh bond and establishes a second. This is similar to the Erasmian interpretation of the exception clause that teaches that adultery before a second marriage dissolves the one flesh bond and allows those who are married the right to divorce and enter into a second marriage. Jesus clearly stated that not only can people commit adultery by having sexual relations outside of the marriage bond but also a second marriage constitutes adultery. Both are considered adultery and neither excuses a second marriage. There is no biblical evidence to support the claim that a second marriage annuls or dissolves the first one.

The nature of sin must also be taken into consideration when considering the durative or progressive nature of the adultery committed by a second marriage. It has already been established that a second marriage is considered adultery. There is no biblical evidence to support the claim that it does not continue to be adultery. If it is believed that it does not constitute a permanent or persistent state of adultery then there are only two options: 1) It is a one time act of adultery where upon committing this sin it instantaneously ceases to be sin. This is twisted logic since committing a sin once cannot cause it to cease being sin. 2) It is a one time act of adultery where upon after committing this sin it slowly ceases to be sin. This is also twisted logic since committing a sin cannot cause it to slowly go away. Sin neither instantaneously ceases nor slowly diminishes by continuing in it.

Conclusion

The only logical and consistently biblical conclusion is that since sexual relations committed upon entering into a second marriage are considered adultery they remain so throughout the entire relationship. It is not only whether the present indicative should be taken as progressive or aoristic it is the nature of the biblical one flesh bond and the nature of sin. Nothing can break the one flesh bond except for death. Sin committed continues to be sin until it is ceased and repented of. There is no other consistent or logical conclusion.

Persistent Sin and Church Discipline

There are no specific verses in the New Testament on how to apply the teachings of Jesus and Paul concerning remarriage and adultery in the local church. This is because the Bible does not give steps in dealing with each specific sin. What the New Testament does teach is broad commands and principles that apply to all sins. The basic New Testament concept is that a professing believer is called to repent of their sin and forsake it. Admit it and quit it, if you will.

If a person persists in living in unrepentant sin the church is to place that person under church discipline until they forsake their sin. The goal of such discipline is to restore the person to fellowship with God and with the local church. This may seem strange to many as the practice of church discipline is almost unheard of in the modern evangelical church. Nevertheless, church discipline is clearly taught in the New Testament.

In Matthew 18:15–20 the steps of discipline include a private meeting, the involvement of one or two others as witnesses, and finally an announcement to the entire local assembly. If a sinning brother or sister remains unrepentant the congregation is to treat that person as an unbeliever. Since the person refuses to live like a believer they are to be treated as an unbeliever. Christians are to judge actions not hearts. The only way to know whether a person may or may not be a believer is by the way they live. If they persist in acting like an unbeliever they should be treated as such. This means they are to be loved by the Christians and have the good news of Christ presented to them. Since the fellowship of the local church is not the place for unbelievers they should not be received into fellowship.

There are some who fall into sin ignorantly. In these instances a spiritually mature believer is to encourage them to make things right with the Lord. These people are to be restored with a spirit of gentleness (Gal. 6:1). There are others who persist in ungodliness and they are to be removed from fellowship (Matt 16:17). It may also be necessary to turn them over to Satan for the destruction of the flesh so their soul may be saved (1 Cor. 5:1–13). Those who are in positions of leadership are to be rebuked publicly so that others may be fearful of following in their sinful ways (1 Tim. 5:19–22).

What does the subject of church discipline have to do with divorce and remarriage? The New Testament teaches that remarriage after divorce is adultery. Those who live in unrepentant adultery are subject to church discipline. Even those who follow the teachings of Erasmus and allow for remarriage after divorce in cases of adultery will need to deal with this topic. Many Christians divorce with adultery playing no part in their separation. If they remarry they commit adultery and Scripture teaches that believers are not to associate with sexually immoral people in the church and the wicked are to be expelled (1 Cor. 5:9–12).

Consistent Application of the Doctrine of Repentance

There are two schools of thought when it comes to the subject of dealing with those who commit adultery by remarrying after divorce. Some claim that since the subject of how to deal with individuals in this situation is not specifically addressed in the New Testament then those who commit adultery by remarrying after divorce should see their current relationship with their new partner as now being God's will for their lives. The problem with this view is two fold. First, it condones adultery. It allows a person to sin without further expectation that they cease from such sin. Jesus claimed that those who divorce and remarry commit adultery. If remarriage is considered to be an adulterous relationship then to continue in it is to continue in sin. Second, it may actually encourage divorced people to remarry. If it is believed that a second marriage now becomes God's will for one's life then people may treat it as a free pass to sin. If they can just reach the "safe platform" of remarriage then they are secure in that relationship and are never expected to alter their actions. It certainly is not unheard of for people to admit that remarriage is wrong but once they commit adultery by remarrying they feel secure in that sinful relationship.

Others claim that since the subject of how to deal with individuals who have remarried after divorce is not specifically addressed in the New Testament then those who commit adultery by remarrying after divorce should be treated differently than those who commit other forms of sin. It should be noted that the New Testament does not specifically address the subject of how to deal with professing believers who commit homosexual acts, engage in premarital sex, or a multitude of other sins. The only sexual sin that is specifically addressed with regard to church discipline is incest (1 Cor. 5). It is assumed that other sexual sins should be dealt with in the same manner as this case of incest.

The Bible teaches that believers are to cease and desist from all acts of known sin. Adultery committed by remarrying is not a greater form of sexual sin, but it also is not a lesser form of sin that need not be discontinued simply because the New Testament does not specifically address it. The church is to proclaim the consistent application of the doctrine of repentance and the forsaking of one's sin. If one is truly repentant they will change their mind about that subject and then subsequently change their actions.

Questions and Applications

Now that the basic groundwork has been laid concerning the subject of divorce, remarriage, and the permanence of adultery the following section will deal with commonly asked questions and practical applications of this doctrine. It is one thing to form doctrinal positions. It is another to lovingly apply biblical doctrine to people's lives. Doctrine and theology were never meant to be divorced from application. Doctrine was intended to be married with practice. The book of James warns Christians to not simply be hearers of the word, but also doers. If we do not practice what we hear we are said to deceive ourselves (Jas. 1:22).

It is understood that some of the ramifications of the Lord's teachings on this subject are difficult and may seem harsh from the human perspective. I myself have thought that things would be easier had the Lord not taught that remarriage after divorce was adultery. It is for this very reason that some believe that remarriage after divorce is not adultery at all. They realize the ramifications of the Lord's teaching about divorce and remarriage and believe that it is too difficult to apply.

Christians need to be educated on the permanence of marriage and the sin of remarriage after divorce. Couples need to be taught that they need to stay together and forgive one another when tough times come. Faithfulness to God and His word requires teaching and applying the whole counsel of God. This is a biblical issue with biblical answers.

Is remarriage after a divorce a greater sin than other sexual sins?

Not necessarily. The reason that this subject is so relevant for the church today is that it is so prevalent. It is causing wide spread damage to society, individual homes, and local fellowships. It is a sin that is commonly practiced in the church and some are diligently working to not only allow this sin but even promote it in certain instances.

Most Christians would never think to teach that pornography, premarital sex, or homosexuality are biblically justified. But when it comes to divorce and remarriage, which Jesus calls adultery, the sin is usually either ignored or justified.

Does divorce make one single again?

No, Romans 7:3 clearly states that neither divorce nor remarriage ends the first marriage. Only death ends marriage. Divorce is a legal action invented by man. There is no place in the Bible which explicitly states that God commands or condones divorce and remarriage for biblically established and consummated marriages. God did not have a plan B in the Garden of Eden for Adam and Eve to divorce and remarry if their marriage did not work out.

The church as well as civil government may oversee the establishment of marriage. The church cannot grant a legal divorce, this action belongs only to the state. Divorce can end the legal aspect of marriage but it can never end the one flesh aspect established by God.

Divorce does not make a man or woman single again. Divorce does not end a person's first marriage. Jesus claimed that remarriage after divorce is adultery. Adultery can only occur if one or both persons involved are married. If two single persons enter into an illicit sexual relationship it would be called fornication not adultery. If both parties in a second marriage were truly single Jesus would not have called their marriage adultery. Jesus taught that when a man marries a divorced woman he commits adultery with her, meaning that he is having sexual relations with another man's wife. Man's civil action in divorce court does not end the one flesh and one spirit aspect of marriage that God has joined together.

If a person divorces before they come to Christ, may they remarry after becoming a believer?

The answer to this is a difficult "No." The Bible makes no distinction whether a divorce occurs before or after regeneration. This is because marriage is universal and based upon the ordinances of creation. It is not specifically a Christian institution. Marriage is a union which is recognized and validated by God. It does not matter whether the marriage is solemnized by the church or by the state or whether the two individuals are believers or unbelievers. Some have attempted to use Second Corinthians 5:17 as a proof text:

> Therefore if any man be in Christ, he is a new creature: old things
> are passed away: behold, all things are become new. (2 Cor. 5:17)

This verse teaches that at the point of conversion a person is a new creature in Christ. It does not teach that the believer is allowed to remarry or commit any other sin. In context it teaches exactly the opposite. The believer is a new creation and the indwelling Holy Spirit of God enables him to obey the commands of Christ. It is true that at salvation all sins are completely forgiven. Forgiveness does not necessarily release one from the consequences of their past. Nothing occurs at salvation that could be construed to teach that one's marital status changes when they place their faith in Christ.

Is remarriage necessary to lead a fulfilled life?

Many who have never married are able to lead a fulfilled life in Christ. Divorced people who do not remarry can find satisfaction and fulfillment by remaining celibate. In western culture marriage has become a form of self gratification. True satisfaction and fulfillment are found only in obeying Christ as Lord. Our society places an emphasis on the pursuit of happiness; the Bible places an emphasis on the pursuit of holiness. If we first seek God's righteousness He will amply supply our needs according to His will.

Western society also places an emphasis on sexual gratification and self realization. Neither of these are biblical concepts. Some appeal to verses like First Corinthians 7:9, "It is better to marry than to burn," which speaks of widows and widowers, as a basis for remarriage after divorce. Paul is clear that separated or divorced believers are to remain unmarried or be reconciled to their spouse (1 Cor. 7:11).

The story of Joseph and Potiphar's wife and the teachings in Romans 6–8 show us that God has given us control over these areas of our lives. Christians are not enslaved to sexual passions. Beyond this many Christians who have never married can testify to the fulfillment they have outside of sexual areas in their lives.

Geoffrey Bromiley has captured the spirit of the New Testament when he writes:

> In a world of the fall the redemptive work of God carries with it
> a service of God not necessarily a technical ministry but a service
> according to God's will, by God's appointment, and in God's disci-
> pleship which means that some part of life, if not all, must be lived
> temporarily outside the regular patterns of God's created order.

This reminds us of the order of priorities which Jesus demands in the calling of His disciples. What God requires must come before all else, the good as well as the bad. The followers of Jesus must be ready, should He will, to renounce even marriage for the sake of the gospel. They must be ready to obey God and not remarry after separation even though they might plead, as they often do, that they have a right to happiness and fulfillment of natural desires. To talk of a right to happiness is to delude one's self. Happiness, when attained, is a gift from God and it cannot be attained, nor can life be fulfilled, where there is a conflict with God's stated will or a defiant refusal to see that true happiness and fulfillment lie only in a primary commitment to God's kingdom and righteousness. For God's sake, some may have to put it in a new perspective, and some who have broken their marriage may have to refrain from marriage. Marriage is a good thing but it is not the "one thing needful" (Luke 10:42). Hence it may be, and in some instances it may have to be, surrendered.

Does time change things?

Some wrongly assume that time changes one's marital status. It is true that God's grace combined with time can heal damaged emotions. The Bible gives no hint that a "period of healing" changes one's marital status to allow a divorced person the freedom to remarry. It is also not true that the state of adultery that is entered into by remarrying after a divorce slowly goes away. If remarriage is considered adulterous one day after a divorce it is still considered adulterous one year or ten years after divorce. The one flesh bond continues on until the death of either partner.

Does grace change things?

God's grace does not make an unrighteous act righteous. Paul makes it clear that believers should not continue to sin so that grace may increase (Rom. 6:1). Paul also reminded the Corinthian believers that some of them *were* fornicators, idolaters, adulterers, and homosexuals. Notice the text does not say that some of them *are*. Their lives had been changed by the grace of God. Those who *were* fornicators no longer practiced that sin; those who were adulterers no longer practiced that sin; those who *were* homosexuals no longer practiced that sin.

In First Corinthians 11 Paul tells the Corinthians that they were washed, they were sanctified, they were justified. The statements are given in reverse order of the Christian experience. Justification and positional sanctification are acts of God which take place when a person places their faith in Christ. Justified (*edikaiothete*) and sanctified (*egiasthete*) use the passive voice of the verb to show that the action was done to them when they believed. Washed (*apelousasthe*) uses the middle voice to show that the believers had washed themselves. Washed speaks of separation from a sinful past, not the washing of salvation. In other words they had left behind their sinful lifestyles which included the above mentioned sexual sins. The grace of God had been poured out on these believer's lives. Because of the work of God they separated themselves from their sinful lifestyles. They did not continue to sin so that the grace of God would increase.

Does adultery or remarriage sever the original one flesh bond?

It is sometimes taught that adultery or the subsequent remarriage after divorce breaks the one flesh bond. Some claim that it is one act of adultery that severs the marriage relationship. Some claim that persistent adultery severs the marriage relationship. Some claim that it is the actual legal divorce that severs the marriage relationship. Others claim that the marriage relationship is severed by a subsequent remarriage to another person. The Bible considers all these acts wrong but it does not teach that any of them sever the marriage relationship.

The error occurs partly because of a misunderstanding as to when the beginning of marriage actually occurs. Marriage takes place at the point in time when the bride and groom signify their commitment to one another. The precise manner may vary from culture to culture but marriage begins at this point. This is most likely the "leaving" spoken of in Scripture. It is this commitment to one another that *allows* them to consummate the marriage with sexual relations. This is most likely the "cleaving" spoken of in Scripture. A misunderstanding takes place when it is believed that sexual relations commence a marriage. Sexual relations do not begin a marriage and sexual relations do not end a marriage. In western culture there may be instances where a couple commit to one another in a legal and binding marriage relationship but never consummate the marriage. In this case they are still married until death do they part. The situation may be somewhat different in Eastern cultures that practice betrothal.

Some mistakenly believe that First Corinthians 6:16 shows that the one flesh bond ceases to exist when a man commits adultery. First, the text says nothing about whether the man is married or not. Second, the text states that the man is "one body" (*soma*) with the harlot not "one flesh" (*sarka*). There is a difference. The first speaks of being united in an illegitimate physical relationship with a harlot and no more. The second speaks of being united in a legitimate physical, emotional, and possibly even spiritual relationship with one's wife.

If it is believed that the one flesh bond ceases to exist when a man commits adultery with a harlot then the next question that must be asked is whether the man is now "one flesh" with the harlot? The text specifically states that he is only "one body" with her. Once again there is no reference to the man being married. For sake of argument if it is believed that adultery ends the one flesh union that a man has with his wife and establishes a one flesh union with the harlot then this would cause the man to cease being married to his wife and marry him to the harlot. If he then returned to his wife and had sexual relations with her he would then be committing adultery against the harlot by having sexual relations with his wife. This is absurd but these are the logical conclusions one would arrive at if they believe that this passage teaches that adultery ends the one flesh bond.

Some erroneously teach that it is persistent adultery that severs the one flesh bond and thus allows a person to divorce their spouse and subsequently remarry. Not only does this view lack scriptural support but the term *persistent* is vague and indefinable. Jesus told His disciples to forgive those who sin against them seventy times seven. This statement of hyperbole means to forgive no matter how many times one is wronged. Paul told husbands to love their wives as Christ loved the church. This is unconditional love. The Bible teaches persistent forgiveness of an adulterous spouse, not divorce of the persistently adulterous spouse.

The persistent adultery theory has other inconsistencies. Either one act of adultery does or does not sever the marriage relationship. To claim anything else is illogical. If one act of adultery severs the one flesh marriage bond then those who commit one act of adultery would cease to be married to their spouse; unless they were to remarry their original spouse. This would mean that the married couple would be living in persistent adultery if one partner committed adultery and the other never knew of it. This is absurd, but sometimes absurdity is necessary to illustrate the absurd.

Others teach that adultery is wrong, divorce is wrong, and remarriage is wrong but since a person is now remarried this makes it right. This safe harbor theory has no biblical basis. It is the admission of sin with no practical application of the doctrine of repentance.

What about civil divorce courts?

The Bible makes it clear that a believer in Christ is not to take another believer to court (1 Cor. 6:1–7). If a dispute arises between a Christian husband and a Christian wife the matter should be judged by other spiritually minded believers. A case can be made that if a believer gets a summons to appear in court because their spouse is pursuing a divorce they should obey the laws of the land and appear in court. One purpose for appearing should be to see if reconciliation of the marriage can be achieved. A Christian should not be the instigator or aggressor of a divorce in a civil court.

Is God's blessing on a second marriage evidence of His approval?

God does not bless that which he considers to be sin. God is good to the righteous and the unrighteous alike. God has mercy on sinners. It is the goodness of God that leads to repentance. Some believe that compatibility or harmony in a second marriage is the sign of God's approval. This misunderstanding of marriage is based upon selfish gratification rather than a life long commitment. Outward circumstances are not the determinant of right and wrong. Some second marriages appear to go quite smoothly. Many carry doubt and guilt. Some are filled with strife and end in a second divorce. Final judgment is rendered in the next life after death.

What if a remarried person recognizes their error?

They should confess their sin to God and be assured that He is faithful and just to forgive them (1 John 1:9). Forgiveness should be sought of those who were harmed or offended. In some cases restitution may be necessary.

The word repentance (*metanoia*) literally means to change one's mind. Part of repentance is to forsake one's sin. Admit it and quit it, if you will. The Bible knows nothing of being sorry for one's sin and still continuing in it. If a person is involved in homosexuality, repentance would include acknowledging that it is wrong, as well as ceasing homosexual behavior. If a person is a thief, they are to admit that stealing is wrong and cease.

The question naturally arises whether remarried Christians should discontinue the relationship they are in. This is a difficult question that is not specifically addressed in the New Testament. Since the one flesh bond is never broken by divorce, the logical implication seems to be that a remarried person should terminate the current relationship. The Lord calls remarriage after divorce adultery. There is no biblical reason to believe that this is a one time act of adultery with no further implications. If it was adulterous in the first instance it remains such throughout the relationship.

May the repentant person return to their former spouse?

If a person involved in a remarriage relationship was previously married and there is a mutual desire on the part of the original partners to be reunited, there is no New Testament principle that forbids it. This is the logical conclusion based upon the continuance of the one flesh bond. For those who are divorced against their will or those who have divorced and recognize their error and subsequently desire to be reunited with their legitimate spouse they should never give up hope. God can work in the hardest of hearts to bring them to repentance.

The Bible teaches that the first marriage remains intact. This is the reason the repentant person may return to their former spouse. The Lord Jesus Christ taught that the so called "second marriage" is adultery. In order to commit adultery one must be married to someone; that someone is the original spouse. One cannot commit adultery if they are not considered married. Jesus claimed that a second marriage is adultery committed against one's spouse. This implies that the divorced person is still married to their original partner.

The laws of men allow legitimate subsequent marriages. The law of Christ does not. The implication of Jesus' teaching is that the person who is granted a civil divorce and then remarries is still married to their original partner in the eyes of God. The two are still one flesh whatever sexual relations either one may have had in the mean time. All additional sexual relations committed are seen as adulterous in the eyes of the Lord. It is for this reason that the repentant person may return to their former spouse because in the eyes of the Lord they did not cease to be married.

Deuteronomy 24:1–4 does raise a question for some. Verse 4 teaches that the first husband who divorced his wife was never allowed to receive her back even if her second husband died. The issue is whether this verse applies to Christians today. If it does apply then this would preclude the divorced spouse from returning. There are many things written in the Old Testament which do not apply to Christians. This may be one of them.

What if a person has counseled others to divorce and remarry?

If a person encourages someone else to sin they should confess it to God and ask the person whom they have counseled to forgive them. They should admit their error and give correct counsel to the individual. Teaching another person to break one of God's commands is a serious matter and should not be taken lightly (Matt. 5:19). The Evangelical church has become enamored with so called "Christian Counseling." The sincere desire to help people is an admirable goal. Erroneous or misguided counsel can hurt people more than help them. All counseling should have its source, method, and conclusions rooted in Scripture. Every counselor, whether personal or professional, should first begin with the question: What does the word of God teach about this subject?

Many counselors are so eager to help hurting people that they will counsel a person to remarry no matter what the circumstances behind the divorce. They just want the person to be "happy." To others, every divorce is different and one is usually encouraged to remarry based upon various subjective criteria such as how long one has been divorced or whether they have had time to "heal." It is not uncommon for divorced women to be told to remarry for the financial sake of the children or that they should remarry in order to fulfill their emotional "needs." There are no verses in Scripture that teach that a woman who does not have children commits adultery if she remarries but if she does have children she does not commit adultery. What if the woman has adequate financial means to support her children and herself? What if the husband has custody of the children?

Those who base their decisions on these and other subjective criteria are practicing a form of situational ethics. Compassion for people is a good thing but answers should be rooted in the authority of Scripture whenever possible. Those who teach that people should remarry because they are "unfulfilled" are subjecting the word of God to a form of moral relativism. The answers to divorce and remarriage questions are to be found inside not outside of Scripture.

Some divorced people remarry because the local church is not functioning in the manner in which God intended it. This is no excuse for sin but local congregations must stand ready to spiritually, emotionally, and financially support divorced people in need, especially those who have children.

What if the elders of a congregation encourage divorce and remarriage?

It is common to hear people claim that since this is a tough subject the elders of each local assembly should examine each case and give approval or disapproval for divorce and remarriage. One problem with this form of thinking is that what is sin and forbidden by "God" in one congregation is not sin and allowed by "God" in another congregation. God is not ambivalent.

Elders are established to shepherd the flock by teaching and upholding God's word. Elders have no more authority to say that a person can divorce and remarry than the Roman Catholic Church has the right to grant annulments. Both are extra-biblical teachings of men with no Scriptural basis.

Is divorce allowed for cruelty or abuse?

Jesus allowed divorce for one reason only, fornication (*porneia*). It is adding to God's word to claim that this includes physical or emotional abuse. The continuation of marriage is always God's will. Separation is allowed (and may be advisable) in situations where one's safety is involved. Any such separation should be taken as a step towards reconciliation of the marriage. Paul clearly states that the wife who departs should be reconciled to her husband or remain single (1 Cor. 7:11).

Should divorced Christians remarry in order to help them resist sexual temptation?

This way may seem right but it is not God's will for the Christian. Since remarriage after divorce is considered adultery then it would make no sense to remarry in order to fulfill one's sexual desires. In doing so one would be committing adultery so that they would not be tempted to commit adultery. Any sexual relations with another person while one's original spouse is alive would be considered adultery. It makes no difference if further sexual relations are committed inside or outside the confines of a subsequent civil marriage ceremony. Further sexual relations are considered adultery either way.

As stated before, even Erasmian interpreters will have to deal with this subject as most divorces between Christians do not occur because of persistent adultery. Even if it is granted that the "exception clause" allows for divorce and remarriage in limited instances, the vast majority of divorces are not covered by the exception clause.

Should divorced Christians remain in a second marriage if they have produced children?

The statement of Jesus that remarriage after a divorce is considered adultery does not mention an "exception" for those who have produced children. The sexual relations between the two are considered adulterous regardless of whether they have children or not. Sin has consequences. Children are harmed when first marriages are granted civil divorces. Children are harmed when they are born out of wedlock. Such consequences remind us of the gravity of sin.

Those who allow divorce and remarriage rarely take into consideration whether the original legitimate marriage produced children. They claim the right to "end" that relationship regardless of whether children were produced or not. It is only when there is talk of ending the second adulterous marriage that concern for children is considered.

This naturally leads to a second question: if a couple repents of their adultery and separates, what should be done for the benefit of the children? Both parents are responsible for the support and upbringing of children which are produced. This is similar to when children are produced out of wedlock before a legitimate marriage. Both persons are responsible for their actions. It would also be similar to a married man who fathers a child during an adulterous affair; he is responsible for the financial and emotional support of that child.

Some have suggested that remarried couples should cease sexual relations but continue to live under the same roof in a brother sister relationship. This may be one alternative; but it is probable that sexual temptation would be too great and one's testimony would be harmed by outward appearances.

May a divorced and remarried person be received into fellowship?

Those who repent and forsake their sin may be received into fellowship. It should be kept in mind that many have been encouraged to remarry by other Christians. This does not excuse the sin but those who are remarried may be seen in two different categories. There who have sinned ignorantly and those who have sinned intentionally. Both sin but the heart is different, especially with those who have remarried before they came to

Christ. Now that they have turned to Christ for forgiveness they should be encouraged to repent and confess their sin to God.

Some may be tempted to ignore this sin especially among those who remarried before turning to Christ. It is sometimes taught that those who divorce and remarry before turning to Christ can continue to live in their sin while those who divorce and remarry after turning to Christ should be subject to church discipline. Although it is true that Christians should know better, the sin is the same. Any sexual relationship that a married person has with anyone other than their original spouse is considered adulterous. A consistent approach teaches that a person involved in an adulterous relationship cannot be received into fellowship. It is most incongruous to teach that a person involved in this kind of adulterous relationship can be received into fellowship while those who are in other adulterous relationships should be disciplined or put out.

Another aspect of this question must be considered: may a divorced but not remarried person be received into fellowship? The answer is generally yes. There is a clear distinction between one who is divorced and one who is divorced and remarried. They are related topics but not one and the same. Remarriage after divorce is adultery. Divorce in and of itself is not necessarily sin. If a person is divorced because their spouse has divorced them against their will then the blame lies with the person who sought the divorce.

What if a Christian friend chooses to divorce and remarry?

First, one should pray for their friend and then for one's self. The emphasis should be for wisdom and love based upon Scripture. The person should go and express Christ's unconditional love to their friend but be prepared to follow Christ no matter what the cost. One should carefully show from Scripture that divorce and remarriage is considered adultery. It is out of concern, not condemnation, that this should be done.

What about vows?

Ecclesiates 5:4 makes it clear that people should keep their vows to God. Most who marry make vows before God that their marriage will be "until death do us part." If the Erasmian position is true then the vows should be changed to read "until adultery, desertion, divorce, or death do us part." For many modern evangelicals it should also read until "irreconcilable differences, lack of emotional support, falling out of love (or almost anything else one wants to add) do us part."

What is God's opinion of divorce?

In Malachi 2:16 God gives His direct opinion of divorce, "He hates" it. Divorce covers a man's garment with wrong. The context of this passage is that the people were weeping and groaning because God would no longer accept their offerings. The reason given for this rejection is that the Israelites were treating their wives treacherously. Three times in Malachi 2:13–16 God states that divorcing one's wife is a form of treachery. Treachery means to betray a trust or loyalty. God states that a wife is the companion from one's youth and that marriage is a covenant. He warns the Jews to take heed to their spirit so that they do not deal treacherously with their wives and betray the covenant of marriage.

Though not expressly restated in the New Testament it is possible that the spiritual principles of this passage may apply to the Christian today. If a Christian divorces his wife and deals treacherously against her it may be possible that God will reject his worship. In First Peter 3:7 husbands are warned to treat their wives with honor or their prayers may be hindered. Certainly divorcing one's wife cannot be considered treating her with honor.

Modern Erasmian interpreters have attempted to explain away this passage by claiming that it is only *hateful* divorces that cover a man's garment with wrong. The Hebrew text literally reads "For He hates sending away." The "He" in this context is God. Modern Erasmian interpreters translate the phrase "For the man who hates and divorces." This is a loose translation at best the purpose of which appears to be to allow divorce and remarriage; except those divorces based upon hate. We are not told the definition of non-hateful divorces which are not considered treacherous. Further proof that the Erasmian understanding of this text is wrong is the contextual statement that the woman is still "thy companion and thy wife by covenant" even after she was divorced.

Did Jesus approve of the Samaritan woman's five marriages?

In John 4:4–26 Jesus encountered the Samaritan woman at Jacob's well. When Jesus told her to call her husband she claimed, "I have no husband." Jesus prophetically replied that she was correct. She had been married to five men and the man she was now with was not her husband. Some have pointed out that Jesus recognized the legality of the woman's five marriages. There is little doubt that Jesus recognized the cultural legality of these marriages. The issue is that Jesus used this to show the woman her sin and her need for a Savior. He was not approving of her multiple marriages any more than He approved of her current unlawful relationship. Her marriages may have been legal according to the civil authorities but they did not receive divine approval. The passage does not teach the dissolution of marriage with the right to remarry. It teaches the sinfulness of the woman who had multiple marriages. It also teaches the love and forgiveness that Christ bestows on all who believe no matter how great their sin.

Are those who teach the permanence of marriage modern day Pharisees?

It is sometimes claimed that those who teach that remarriage after divorce is adultery are similar to the Pharisees of Jesus' day. This analogy has no factual basis. According to the historical record there were few if any Pharisees who taught that a divorced person could not remarry.

In the first century AD the Pharisees were divided into two main camps, those who followed the teachings of Hillel and those who followed the teachings of Shammai. Hillel taught that a person could divorce his wife for almost any reason. Shammai taught that a person could divorce his wife only for serious sexual sins. Both claimed that a divorced person had the right to remarry.

It is actually modern day evangelicals who teach that divorce and remarriage is allowed who are the most like the Pharisees. They debate the nuances of the divorce clause and seek legal loopholes that allow people not only the right to divorce but also to remarry. Some allow divorce and remarriage for almost any reason and while others limit it to serious sexual sins. The words of the Lord Jesus would be the same to these teachers as it was for the Pharisees, *Therefore what God has joined together, let no man separate* (Matt. 19:6).

It is also claimed that to require such a high standard as no remarriage after divorce is legalism. Legalism is defined as attempting to earn or keep one's salvation by works of the Law. Obeying Scripture with a proper heart towards God is not legalism. Nor is it legalism to obey what Christ commands. The balance is found in the command to "speak the truth in love." How Jesus dealt with the woman accused of adultery in John 8:1–11 is a clear example of love without compromise. He did not condemn the woman to death by stoning. He did not lower God's standards. He told her to go and sin no more.

Chapter 6

Husband of "One" Wife

THE NEW Testament lists two offices for the servant leadership of each local congregation, Elder and Deacon. The books of First Timothy and Titus give specific qualifications for men who are to shepherd God's people. The qualifications listed are the minimum standards of what an elder or deacon "must" be. All believing men should seek after these character traits for their lives. Not all will meet these standards and qualify for leadership. Being disqualified from leadership does not mean a man cannot carry on a fruitful ministry for the Lord. The phrase "husband of one wife" has been the subject of much discussion.

Relevant Texts

First Timothy 3:2

Greek	Transliteration	Translation	Parsing
ειναι	(*einai*)	"to be"	pres. inf.
μιας	(*mias*)	"of one"	gen. fem. sing.
γυναικος	(*gunaikos*)	"wife / woman"	gen. fem. sing.
ανδρα	(*andra*)	"husband / man"	acc. masc. sing.

First Timothy 3:12

Greek	Transliteration	Translation	Parsing
εστωσαν	(*estosan*)	"they must be"	pres. act. imp.
μιας	(*mias*)	"of one"	gen. fem. sing.
γυναικος	(*gunaikos*)	"wife / woman"	gen. fem. sing.
ανδρες	(*andres*)	"husbands / men"	nom. masc. pl.

Titus 1:6

Greek	Transliteration	Translation	Parsing
εστιν	(*estin*)	"he is"	pres. act. ind.
μιας	(*mias*)	"of one"	gen. fem. sing.
γυναικος	(*gunaikos*)	"wife / woman"	gen. fem. sing.
ανηρ	(*aner*)	"husband / man"	nom. masc. sing.

Related Texts

First Timothy 5:9

Greek	Transliteration	Translation	Parsing
ενος	(*henos*)	"of one"	gen. masc. sing.
ανδρος	(*andros*)	"husband / man"	gen. masc. sing.
γυνη	(*gune*)	"wife / woman"	nom. fem. sing.

The phrase "husband of one wife" is "*mias*/3391 *gunaikos*/1135 *andra*/435." The literal Greek allows for either "of one wife a husband" or "of one woman a man." Smoothed into modern English the phrase would be "husband of one wife." It could also be a combination of the two such as "of one wife a man."

Some have attempted to translate it as "one woman man" but this is not precise. The numeral "one" (*mias*) is genitive as well as feminine. Since it is genitive it should be translated in the possessive sense. In an English translation this normally requires the use of the word "of." Since it is feminine it modifies the word "woman" or "wife."

In the three relevant texts the substantive *man* is anarthrous, without the article. This is pertinent as translations throughout the centuries have consistently rendered this phrase as "*the* husband of one wife" even though no article is present. The absence of the article can mean that the noun is indefinite but there are also considerable examples in the New Testament where an anarthrous noun should be translated as definite.

Robertson writes:

> We have seen that the substantive may still be definite if anarthrous, though not necessarily so.[1]

---

1. A. T. Robertson, *Grammar of the Greek New Testament*, p. 791.

Examples of this in Paul's letters include First Timothy 5:9, (*henos andros gune*) "*the* wife of one husband" and First Thessalonians 2:13 (*logon theou*) "*the* word of God."

Robertson expands on this:

> It would have been very easy if the absence of the article in Greek always meant that the noun was indefinite, but we have seen that this is not the case. The anarthrous noun may *per se* be either definite or indefinite.[2]

Dana and Mantey write:

> It is important to bear in mind that we cannot determine the English translation by the presence or the absence of the article in Greek. Sometimes we should use the article in the English translation when it is not used in the Greek, and sometimes the idiomatic force of the Greek article may be best rendered by the anarthrous noun in English.[3]

Greek grammar is only part of the equation in translating and interpreting Scripture. The other part of the equation is context. In determining the view of the writer much of the time contextual usage is a deciding factor. Context plays a significant role in translating these three relevant phrases. With few exceptions the phrase has normally been translated "the husband of one wife." This is especially true when translations are undertaken by a group or team of qualified Greek scholars. The KJV, NKJV, RSV, NAS, and NIV all uniformly translate these passages in First Timothy and Titus as "the husband of one wife."

As far back as the 5th century the Latin speaking church translated the phrase "husband of one wife." The Latin Vulgate translates First Timothy 3:2:

unius uxoris virum (of one wife a man)

First Timothy 3:12 and Titus 1:6 are similarly translated. The Latin word for wife is *uxor*. There are other Latin words such as *femina*, *mulier*, and *puella* that the translators would have used if they simply wanted to express the idea of a woman or feminine gender.

Those who wish to allow divorced and remarried men to serve as elders usually resist the translation "husband of one wife." They normally prefer the translation "one woman man." Many who prefer the translation

2. Ibid., p. 796.
3. Dana and Mantey, *Manual Grammar of the Greek New Testament*, p. 150.

"one woman man" fail to admit that the Greek is just as literally translated "husband of one wife." This is because the anarthrous construction, absent the article, can mean that the qualitative aspect of the noun rather than the strict identity of the noun is emphasized.

Dana and Mantey write:

> An object of thought may be conceived of from two points of view: as to identity or quality. To convey the first point of view the Greek uses the article; for the second the anarthrous construction is used.[4]

Those who wish to allow divorced and remarried men to serve as elders frequently claim that the qualitative aspect of the noun emphasizes the current state of the man not lusting after or flirting with other women rather than the sin of a second marriage. In response to this there is nothing inherent about the anarthrous construction that would lead one to this conclusion. In order for the quality of the man to be true his actions must represent his identity.

Dana and Mantey present examples of definite anarthrous constructions which show the qualitative aspect of the noun. They include Ephesians 5:9 (*tekna photos*) "children of light" and First Thessalonians 5:5 (*huioi photos*) "sons of light." Both phrases were penned by Paul. In both of these citations the stress is placed upon the quality of the noun but that which is stated about their identity is nevertheless true.[5]

Blass, Debrunner, and Funk cite an example of the qualitative genitive in First Timothy 5:9 (*me ellattos etos exekonta*) "not less than sixty years."[6] Here is a statement about the *one husband wife* who must be at least sixty years old to be placed on the list of widows. This is not a generalization about her qualities but a substantive statement of her minimum age.

The use of a qualitative genitive in First Timothy 3:2, 3:12, and Titus 1:6 in no way weakens "the husband of one wife" translation. A man's qualities (the things about him) show the distinctives of who he is. The text states that the man who desires the position of elder or deacon must have the distinctive quality of being *mias gunaikos andra*. The translation "one woman man" is permissible but the translation "husband of one wife" is better. This has been the normative and preferred translation of Greek scholars throughout much of church history. In the English speak-

---

4. Ibid., p. 149.

5. Ibid., p. 150.

6. Blass, DeBrunner, and Funk, *Greek Grammar of the New Testament*, p. 99.

ing world this is shown by the overwhelming majority of Bible translations which render the phrase in this manner.

Wuest writes:

> The literal translation is, "a man of one woman." The words, when used of the marriage relation come to mean, "a husband of one wife." The two nouns are without the definite article, which construction emphasizes character or nature.[7]

Although Wuest sees the use of the qualitative genitive as an emphasis on character he does not allow this passage to teach that a divorced and remarried man may serve as an elder or a deacon. This is shown in his translation as well as his exposition. He quotes Alford, Vincent, and White in *Expositors* to support his conclusion. None of these sources allow divorced and remarried men to serve as elders.

Wuest states:

> An interpretive translation offers the rendering, "married only once." We submit that this is not the literal translation of the Greek here, but in light of the above historical background, it is the interpretation of the words, and gives the English reader in unmistakably clear language, the true meaning of the words in the A.V., "the husband of one wife". . . . Since character is emphasized by the Greek construction, the bishop should be a man who loves only one woman as his wife.[8]

Men have come up with five different interpretations of what "*mias gunaikos andra*" in First Timothy and Titus may mean:

1. Elders or Deacons must be married.

2. A remarried widower cannot serve as an Elder or Deacon.

3. A Polygamist cannot serve as an Elder or Deacon.

4. Divorced and remarried men cannot serve as Elders or Deacons.

5. An Elder or Deacon must be faithful to one woman at a time.

These interpretations are not necessarily either/or selections. More than one may be included in the final biblical conclusion. The use of the

---

7. Kenneth Wuest, *Pastoral Epistles*, p. 53. Wuest's statement about "character" is widely quoted by those who wish to allow divorced and remarried men to serve as elders. Most fail to mention that Wuest does not agree with their allowance of this practice.

8. Ibid., p. 55.

word *aner* (man) rather than the word *anthropos* precludes women (*gune*) from serving as elders or deacons.

Elders or Deacons must be married.

This is a doubtful interpretation. The verse states that the man must be the husband of "one" wife not "a" wife. The adjective "one" (*mias*) is in the emphatic position. This means that the emphasis is placed on the number of wives a man is allowed to have, not that he must be married. If Paul wanted to teach that an elder or deacon must be the "husband of a wife" he could have easily expressed himself by the omission of "one" (*mias*). Paul is listing sins or character flaws in a man's life that would disqualify him from leadership. Jesus taught that remarriage after divorce was adultery (Luke 16:18). Neither being married once nor remaining single is a sin (1 Cor. 7:7, 28). Paul claimed that the single life allows a fuller devotion to the Lord (1 Cor. 7:32). He taught that virgins were free to marry (1 Cor. 7:35–36).

Mounce lists other counter arguments as well:

> (b) Paul and Timothy would not be eligible to be overseers; (c) it runs counter to Paul's teaching that being single is a better state for church workers (if they have the gift; 1 Cor. 7:17, 25–38); (d) this line of reasoning, to be consistent, would have to argue that the overseer is required to have more than one child since *tekna* "children" (v. 4) is plural; and (e) most adult men were married so it would have been a moot point.[9]

Chrysostom writes:

> A Bishop then he says "must be blameless the husband of one wife." This he does not lay down as a rule, as if he must not be without one.[10]

A remarried widower cannot serve as an Elder or Deacon.

This view was held by some second and third century commentators. It is improbable that this was what Paul was saying. Paul not only permitted but encouraged younger widows to remarry (I Cor. 7:39–40; I Tim. 5:14). If widows were allowed to remarry it would seem probable that a widower would be allowed to do the same. In the centuries following the apostolic age, remarriage after the death of one's spouse was seen as a weakness but

9. William Mounce, *Word Biblical Commentary*, vol. 46, p. 171.
10. Chrysostom, *Homily X*, First Timothy 3:2.

not a sin. The argument that a second marriage is a sign of spiritual weakness on the part of the elder or deacon could just as well be applied to the first marriage.

The Bible teaches that only death dissolves the one-flesh marriage bond, thus freeing the living spouse to remarry without sinning (1 Cor. 7:39–40; Rom. 7:2–3). The context of First Timothy and Titus deals with sins that would disqualify a man from leadership. Nowhere in Scripture is remarriage after the death of one's wife portrayed as forbidden or even morally questionable.

Mounce writes:

> The later reference (applied to "younger widows") is in the context of Paul's instructions to widows where earlier Paul says that a widow may be enrolled if she has been *enos andros gune*, "one-man woman" (1 Tim. 5:9), the exact phrase applied to overseers and deacons but reversed in gender. Because the phrases are so unusual, we expect them to have the same meaning. It seems doubtful that Paul would encourage the remarriage of "younger widows" if this is meant that they could never later be enrolled if they were again widowed.[11]

The no remarriage for widowers view was held by some 2nd and 3rd century commentators. In the centuries following the apostolic age remarriage after the death of one's spouse was seen as a weakness but not a sin. *The Shepherd of Hermas* reads:

> "If a wife or husband dies, and the widower or widow marries, does he or she commit sin?" "There is no sin in marrying again," said he; "but if they remain unmarried, they gain great honor and glory with the Lord; but if they marry, they do not sin."[12]

Tertullian (a Montanist) writes:

> If it be granted that the second marriage is lawful, yet all things lawful are not expedient.[13]

Cyril of Jerusalem states:

> But folk may be pardoned for contracting a second marriage, lest infirmity end in fornication.[14]

11. William Mounce, *Word Biblical Commentary*, p. 173.
12. *Shepherd of Hermas*, Commandment 4, ch. 4.
13. Tertullian, *De pud.* ch. 8.
14. Cyril, *Catechetical Lectures* 4:26.

The context of this statement shows that Cyril was speaking of remarried widows and widowers not divorce and remarriage.

Chrysostom writes:

> But why does he discourage second marriages? Is the thing condemned? By no means, that is heretical. Only he would have her henceforth occupied in spiritual things, transferring all her care to virtue. For marriage is not an impure state, but one of much occupation.[15]

Montanists forbade second marriages as an article of faith. The "Apostolic Constitutions" allowed a man who was already married to be ordained, but if he was single when he was ordained, he must remain so all his life. It should be noted that not all commentators held that remarriage after the death of a man's wife would disqualify him from church leadership.

Theodoret of Mopsuestia mentions contemporary commentators who allow remarried widowers to be elders and deacons:

> They say (i.e. various interpreters) . . . Likewise any man who lives on after the death of his first wife may legitimately take a second wife, as long as he lives in the same way with her as with the first, and ought not be prohibited from becoming a bishop.[16]

Some claim that it was purely the ascetic tendencies of these early Christians that led them to teach that remarried widowers cannot serve as elders or deacons. The motive behind this is often an attempt to discredit other early church teachings regarding the permanence of marriage. The early church writers had a virtual consensus in teaching that divorced and remarried men could not serve as elders or deacons. They made a distinction between the weakness of remarriage after the death of a spouse and the sin of remarriage after the divorce of a spouse. Modern expositors who wish to allow divorced and remarried men to serve as elders normally down play this historical fact by claiming that *both* conclusions were merely based upon the ascetic tendencies of the early church. In response to this it should be noted that there are still scholars today who believe that the "one wife" statement prohibits remarried widowers from serving as elders and deacons. These modern conclusions can hardly be explained away as the result of ascetic cultural influences.

15. Chrysostom, *Homily XIV*, First Timothy 5:9.
16. Theodoret of Mopsuestia, *Commentary on First Timothy.*

A polygamist cannot serve as an Elder or Deacon.

Some modern commentators teach that the "husband of one wife" statement applies only to polygamists. A man can have as many wives as he wants but only one at a time. He is allowed to divorce and remarry, numerous times, as long as he legally has only one wife at a time. They believe that the main modern day application refers to missionaries who go to a people who practice polygamy. When a man turns to Christ he must cease practicing polygamy if he desires to serve as an elder or deacon. This may be one possible application but it is a doubtful interpretation. The New Testament expects all believers to refrain from polygamy once they turn to Christ. It is doubtful that only those believers who sought positions of oversight would need to abstain from polygamy. It is highly unlikely that Paul's original intent was to deal with converted polygamists. There is no hint in the New Testament that this was a problem that burdened the early church.

Homer Kent writes:

> Polygamy at this time was forbidden in the empire, although some of the Jews were known to have practiced it, and even many Romans found ways to circumvent the law. There is no evidence from these days that any polygamist entered the church. Hence it is hardly to be expected that a special prohibition was needed to exclude them from overseer, since there was probably none in the membership.[17]

Mounce writes:

> Even if polygamy existed among the Jews, evidence is lacking that it was practiced by Christians, and therefore "Christian polygamy" most likely is not in view.[18]

Correct rules can help determine the meaning of Scripture:

1. Interpret in a plain and normal grammatical sense.

2. Interpret obscure passages in light of the clear.

3. Interpret historically and contextually.

4. Cross reference words and phrases with others in the same book or by the same author.

17. Homer Kent, *Pastoral Epistles*, p. 127.
18. William Mounce, *Word Biblical Commentary*, p. 171.

Was Paul dealing with polygamists who were candidates to be elders or deacons? Alford writes:

> But the objection to taking this meaning is that the Apostle would hardly have specified that as a requisite for the episcopate or presbyterate, which we know to have been fulfilled by all the Christians whatever: no instance being adduced of polygamy being practiced in the Christian church, and no exhortations to abstain from it.[19]

Justin Martyr tells us that in the second century AD some Jews still practiced polygamy but he gives no mention that the practice occurred among Gentiles. The historian Will Durant tells us that polygamy was prohibited by Roman law. The lex *Antoniana de civitate* prohibited polygamy among Gentiles but made an exception for Jews. Theodosius enforced monogamy on the Jews (*circa* AD 390) because of their continued practice of polygamy. It is known that some Jews in the East continued to practice polygamy until the establishment of Israel in 1948.

In speaking of his Jewish ancestry Josephus states:

> For it is the ancient practice among us to have many wives at the same time.[20]

Greeks and Romans practiced adultery, fornication, homosexuality, concubinage, as well as divorce and remarriage. If polygamy existed among gentiles it was neither lawful nor common. Paul wrote the epistles to Timothy and Titus in Ephesus and Crete. These were predominantly Gentile Roman communities. These Ephesians and Cretans were excluded from the common wealth of Israel (Eph. 2:12). It seems improbable that they would be involved in the mainly Jewish practice of polygamy. There is no evidence that they practiced polygamy. They did practice divorce and remarriage. It seems more probable that Paul would deal with something that was a problem, divorce and remarriage, rather than something that was not, polygamy. It is also possible that multiple marriages were seen as a form of polygamy.

Oepke writes:

> No laws existed against bigamy but monogamy ruled in practice . . . divorce was common either by consent, by declaration before a judge or third party, or by unilateral action of the husband. Repeated divorces constituted a form of polygamy.[21]

19. Henry Alford, cited by Kenneth Wuest, *Pastoral Epistles*, p. 55.
20. Josephus, *Antiquities of the Jews*, Book 17, ch. 1, Sec. 2.
21. A. Oepke, *gune Theological Dictionary of the New Testament*, p. 134.

Divorced and remarried men cannot serve as elders or deacons.

This seems to be included in Paul's prohibition. Since this is a difficult passage, it would be wise to cross reference it with similar words or phrases made in the same book. In First Timothy 5:9, Paul gives instructions on who may be placed on the list of widows to receive financial support. He states that qualified widows must have been the "wife of one husband." The original phrase is *"henos/1520 andros/435 gune/1135."* This is the same phrase, exactly reversed, as in First Timothy 3:2, 3:12; and Titus 1:6. The words *"andros"* and *"gune"* have the same lexical roots as *"andra"* and *"gunaikos"* in First Timothy 3. The only variation is that *"henos"* is genitive masculine while *"mias"* is genitive feminine. Both words should be translated "of one."

Tertullian writes:

> When he suffers not men twice married to preside (over a church), when he would not grant a widow into the order unless she had been "the wife of one man."[22]

William Mounce writes:

> Since the phrase is somewhat unusual, it is safe to insist that it had the same meaning in reverse when applied to widows (1 Tim. 5:9) and there is no evidence of polyandry.[23]

Robertson writes:

> The wife of one man (*henos andros gune*). Widows on this list must not be married a second time.[24]

Since "wife of one husband" excludes women who had divorced and remarried, "husband of one wife" would exclude men who had divorced and remarried. It is doubtful that Paul was excluding women who had previously been widowed and remarried. Remarriage after the death of one's husband was not considered a sin. Paul actually encourages younger widows to remarry (I Tim. 5:14). It is improbable that Paul was dealing with polyandry, being legally married to more than one husband at a time. There is no record that this was practiced by women in New Testament times.

22. Tertullian, *To His Wife*, ch. 6.
23. William Mounce, *Word Biblical commentary*, p. 171.
24. A. T. Robertson, *Word Pictures in the New Testament*, vol. IV, p. 585. Robertson contradicts his own reasoning when interpreting First Timothy 3:2, 12.

Some claim the use of *present* tense Greek verbs in First Timothy 3 and Titus 1 allows divorced and remarried men to be placed in leadership. The *present* tense is primarily used to show the idea of progress. It is generally, though not exclusively, a durative tense. It is used in First Timothy 3 and Titus 1 when giving the necessary qualifications for those who desire to be in leadership. It is erroneous to believe the use of the *present* tense allows divorced and remarried men to be elders or deacons.

The interpretation of First Timothy 3 and Titus 1 does not hinge on the use of *present* tense verbs. Rather, it hinges on the permanence of marriage. The marriage bond is not dissolved by adultery, divorce, or any other thing short of death. The man who divorces and remarries, is actually taking a second wife. He is the husband of *more* than one wife.

Athenagoras writes:

> That a person should either remain as he was born or be content with one marriage; for a second marriage is only a specious adultery. "For whoever puts away his wife," says He, "and marries another, commits adultery."[25]

Justin Martyr writes:

> Whosoever marry her that is divorced from another husband, commits adultery . . . So that all who by human law, are twice married, are in the eyes of our Master sinners, and those who look upon a woman to lust after her.[26]

Origen writes:

> But as a woman is an adulteress, even though she seem to be married to a man, while the former husband is still living, so also the man who seems to marry her who has been put away does not so much marry her as commit adultery with her according to the declaration of our Savior.[27]

Augustine writes:

> Seeing that the compact of marriage is not done away with by divorce intervening; so that they continue as wedded persons one to another, even after separation; and commit adultery with those,

25. Athenagoras, *A Plea for Christians*, ch. XXXIII. Vincent (*Word Studies* 4:229) cites the "specious adultery" phrase as a reference to the remarriage of widowers. Vincent is clearly in error. The Scriptural quotation and the context of the statement show that Athenagoras was referring to divorce and remarriage.

26. Justin Martyr, *First Apology*, ch. 15.

27. Origen, *Commentary on Matthew*, ch. 14.

with whom they shall be joined, even after their own divorce, whether the woman with the man, or the man with the woman.[28]

Stauffer writes:

> Dissolution may take place but not a new marriage, for the replacement of one spouse by another is adultery and affects the original union.[29]

Some allow a man who was divorced and remarried, before he came to Christ, to be an elder or deacon. It is assumed that God's forgiveness clears the slate for the man to be in leadership. It is true that God forgives all sin and releases each believer from guilt and eternal punishment. There are consequences for sin in this life. If pressed to its logical conclusion, then all divorced men, who confess their sin of divorce and remarriage, may become elders or deacons. It would not matter whether it happened before or after conversion. An elder could divorce his wife and remarry. He could ask forgiveness and be reinstated to leadership. He could then divorce and start the cycle all over again.

Augustine has this to say:

> On this account the Sacrament of marriage of our time hath been so reduced to one man and one wife, as that it is not lawful to ordain any as a steward of the Church, save the husband of one wife. And this they have understood more acutely who have been of opinion, that neither is he to be ordained, who as a catechumen or as a heathen had a second wife.[30]

Augustine claimed that the man who had been married a second time was not allowed to be an Elder in the church. Augustine made no distinction whether the man was a catechumen or a heathen (*i.e.* before he was saved or after he was saved).

Chrysostom writes:

> "A Bishop then," he says, "must be blameless, the husband of one wife." This he does not lay down as a rule, as if he must not be without one. But as prohibiting his having more than one. For even the Jews were allowed to contract second marriages, and even to have two wives at one time.[31]

28. Augustine, *On the Good of Marriage*, sec. 7.

29. E. Stauffer, *gameo Theological Dictionary of the New Testament*, p. 112.

30. Augustine, *On the Good of Marriage*, sec. 21.

31. Chrysostom, *Homily X, First Timothy 3:2*.

Chrysostom knew that Jews not only practiced polygamy, but also divorced and remarried. Both actions would mean a man had more than one wife. Both would disqualify a man from leadership.

Ambrose writes:

> And the Apostle has established a law, saying: "If any man be without reproach the husband of one wife . . ." he, however, who has married again has no guilt of pollution, but is disqualified for the priestly prerogative . . . But we must first notice that not only has the Apostle laid down this rule concerning the bishop or priest, but that the Fathers in the Nicene Council added that no one who has contracted a second marriage ought to be admitted among the clergy at all.[32]

Ambrose takes the idea of clergy farther than the New Testament allows. Nevertheless the consensus opinion of the early church regarding leadership and those who have contracted second marriages is represented here. The context of Ambrose' statement refers mostly to widowers remarrying but is also forbids those who are married a second time because of divorce.

Adam Clarke writes:

> He must be the husband of one wife. He should be a married man, but he should be no polygamist; and have only one wife . . . The apostle's meaning appears to be this: that he should not be a man who has divorced his wife and married another; nor one that has two wives at a time.[33]

The following is a further list of quotes of those who believe that Paul excludes those who are divorced and remarried from serving as elders and deacons by the phrase "husband of one wife."

Basil:

> The canon absolutely excludes digamists from the ministry.[34]

The context of this letter deals with divorce and remarriage not the remarriage of widowers.

The Theological Dictionary of the New Testament reads:

> The qualification "wife of one husband" may refer to non-remarriage after the death of the spouse, but in view of the right to such

---

32. Ambrose, *Letter LXIII*, sec. 63–64.

33. Adam Clarke, *Notes in First Timothy* 3:2.

34. Basil, *Letter CLXXXVIII*.

remarriage in Rom. 7:1ff., the commendation of it for younger widows (1 Tim. 5:14), and the general approval of married clergy (1 Tim. 3), it seems more likely that the reference is to remarriage after divorce (as in 1 Tim. 3:2, 12).[35]

Derickson writes:

He (Jesus) seems to leave the impression that those that remarry are involved in adultery. Since adultery is intimate relations outside of the bounds of marriage it would seem to be a continuing thing. It does not seem logical that a church would want a man in the position of elder, which was in continuing adultery.[36]

Matthew Henry:

First Timothy 3:2–He must be the husband of one wife; not having given a bill of divorce to one, and then taken another, or not having many wives at once. First Timothy 3:12—As he said before of the bishops of ministers so here of the deacons, they must be the husband of one wife, such had not put away their wives, upon dislike, and married others.

Titus 1:6—The husband of one wife may be either not having divorced his wife and married another (as was too common among those of the circumcision, even for slight causes) or the husband of one wife, that is, one and the same time no bigamist.[37]

John Wesley:

But whereas polygamy and divorce on slight occasions were common both among Jews and heathen, it teaches us that ministers, ought to stand clear of those sins.[38]

John Gill:

Only if he marries or is married, that he should have but one wife at a time; so that this rule excludes all such persons from being elders, or pastors, or overseers of the churches, that were "polygamists;" who had more wives than one at a time, or had divorced their wives, and not for adultery, and had married others.[39]

---

35. A. Oepke, *gune Theological Dictionary of the New Testament*, p. 136.

36. Stanley Derickson, *Notes on Theology*, p. 1087.

37. Matthew Henry, *Commentaries in First Timothy and Titus*.

38. John Wesley, *Notes on First Timothy*.

39. John Gill, *Commentary on First Timothy*.

Adam Clarke:

> The apostle's meaning appears to be this: that he should not be a man who has divorced his wife and married another; nor one that has two wives at a time.[40]

Newport White:

> What is here forbidden is digamy under any circumstances. This view is supported (a) by the general drift of the qualities required here in a bishop; (b) by the corresponding requirement in a church widow, v. 9, and (c) by the practice of the early church (Apostolic Constitutions, vi. 17; Apostolic Canons 16 (17); Tertullian, *ad Uxorem*, I. 7: *de Monogam.* 12; *de Exhort. Castitatis*, cc. 7, 13: Athenagoras, *Legat.* 33; Origen, *in Lucam*, xvii. P. 953, and the Canons of the councils, e.g., Neocaesarea (A.D. 314) can. 7. Quinisext. Can. 3).[41]

Marvin Vincent (*Word Studies in the New Testament*):

> The husband of one wife. Compare verse 12; Titus 1:6. Is the injunction aimed (a) at immoralities respecting marriage—concubinage, etc., or (b) at polygamy, or (c) at remarriage after death or divorce? The last is probably meant.[42]

Homer Kent:

> Consequently, when men were to be considered for this high office, there must be no record of divorce or other marital infidelity in the candidate, even before his conversion. The same marital standard was true of the enrolled widow as of the overseer (3:2) and the deacon (3:12). There must have been no divorce, polyandry, or other marital adulteration.[43]

Charles Ryrie:

> Clearly this is not a prohibition against bigamy or polygamy since these were not practiced among the Greeks and Romans. They had multiple women in their lives, but only one wife. It is a question of whether Paul is prohibiting digamy (being married twice legally). Personally I see the evidence as proscribing digamy for an elder.[44]

40. Adam Clarke, *Notes on First Timothy 3:2*.
41. Newport J. D. White, *The Expositor's Greek Testament*, p. 111.
42. Marvin Vincent, *Word Studies in the New Testament*, First Timothy 3:2.
43. Homer Kent, *Pastoral Epistles*, p. 172.
44. Charles Ryrie, *Basic Theology*, p. 416.

Paul Enns:

> Husband of one wife: it does not mean "one at a time" (polygamy was unknown among Greeks and Romans); he has not been divorced and remarried.[45]

Those who assume that God would not require such high standards for leadership should read the Old Testament. In Leviticus 21:7 the sons of Aaron, the priests, were not to marry a harlot or a divorced woman. In Leviticus 21:13–15 the high priest was not to marry a harlot, a widow, or a divorced woman. He must marry a virgin. It is admitted that believers today are not regulated by the Levitical law. It is also acknowledged that the passage does not restrict divorced men from serving as priests, but rather those who had married a divorced woman. Nevertheless, those who assume that God wouldn't disqualify a divorced person from spiritual leadership may be assuming too much.

What if a man is not himself divorced but marries a divorced woman? There are qualifications mentioned in First Timothy and Titus which cover this. The elder is to be blameless. Would an elder who has committed adultery by remarrying a divorced woman be considered blameless? He may be forgiven, but is he blameless? There is a difference!

What if a man was divorced but has not remarried? "Blameless" includes anything in a man's past or present that would bring his character into question. The elder must be one who "rules" his house well. If he cannot govern his own house, he cannot govern the church of God. Even if his wife was the "guilty" party, Scripture states that the wives of leaders must be faithful. The wife of an elder can make or break his ministry. An elder must also have his children in subjection. If a man's children do not live with him because of divorce, how can he claim they are in subjection to him?

Answers to Objections of the no divorce and remarriage view.

Objection—Paul could have used different Greek words to literally state an elder or deacon must not be "divorced and remarried."

Answer—The phrase "husband of one wife" is broader than the proscription of men who were divorced and remarried, yet still includes it. Paul did not use the precise words "not a polygamous." Yet, all agree that the "husband of one wife" phrase would exclude polygamy. He also

---

45. Paul Enns, *Moody Handbook of Theology*, p. 355.

did not utilize the precise words to forbid "adulterers," "fornicators," or "practitioners of concubinage" to serve as elders. The same thing could be said about "homosexuals." The phrase "husband of one wife" prohibits all these sins as well as divorce and remarriage.

Objection—The use of the present tense verb stresses the general qualities of the man and what he currently must be. These qualities are unrelated to sins that he may have committed in the past.

Answer—If the "present tense" objectors were logically consistent then the use of the present tense verb would only apply to those sins that an elder or deacon is presently committing. The "husband of one wife" phrase is unqualified by any particular past tense time limitation. One would be inconsistent if he disqualified a man who divorced and remarried yesterday while allowing a man to serve who divorced and remarried five years ago.

The problem with this objection is further shown by the variations of it. Some claim that these qualifications have no relationship to a man's sins before he became a Christian. Some claim that these qualifications do not apply to a man's sins after he was saved but before he became an elder. Others claim an elder or deacon would only be disqualified if he divorced and remarried after obtaining office in the local church.

The claim is made that God's forgiveness cancels past sins so that a man may hold the office of elder or deacon. If this is true then only those men who are currently practicing these sins would be disqualified. To be completely logical and consistent a man who is an elder or deacon could divorce his wife and remarry. He could then claim God's forgiveness and be reinstated to a position of leadership. A uniform application of this "present tense" teaching would mean that an elder or deacon could divorce and remarry numerous times and continue to be reinstated after each divorce.

In some modern evangelical churches a man who has only one divorce and remarriage may be allowed to serve while those who have more than one divorce and remarriage are not. This shows the fallacy of the position. If qualification for leadership is based only on the "present tense" then men who have multiple marriages, even after they become Christians, would be qualified to serve as elders and deacons. The truth is that one divorce and remarriage, whenever it occurred, disqualifies the man from church oversight. This is because the man who divorces and remarries actually has two wives. This is true whether the divorce and remarriage occurred before or after the man was saved. Being born again does not change one's marital status.

When a man and a woman are married they become "one flesh." They are united by a bond that can only be broken by death. Romans 7 and First Corinthians 7 teach that the wife is bound to her husband as long as he lives. Matthew 5, Luke 16, and Mark 10 teach that divorce and remarriage is equal to adultery. When a man divorces his wife the court may claim that they are no longer married but the Bible teaches that they remain "one flesh" (Matt. 19:6). In Mark 6:17–18 Herodias remarried Herod yet the Bible claims that Herodias was still the wife of Philip even though her remarriage was legal according to Roman law. The phrase "husband of one wife" can only allow for divorce and remarriage if all divorces have the exact same effect as death.

Objection—The no divorce and remarriage position is the only qualification that is related to a man's past.

Answer—This is a further variation of the "present tense" objection. There are other things in the leadership qualifications of First Timothy and Titus that take into account a man's past. Being blameless (1 Tim. 3:2) and having a good reputation (1 Tim. 3:7) are the result of years of honest dealing and integrity. The "present tense" advocates often fail to take this into account when they claim that *today* (the present) is all that matters. A dishonest man may need to make restitution for sins that he committed years earlier. Simply claiming that these sins occurred before a man was saved would not mean that he had a good reputation with those outside the church. Managing one's household (1 Tim. 3:4) and having faithful children (Titus 1:6) is the culmination of years of labor. The failure of a man to manage his household disqualifies him from leadership.

Derickson writes:

> A man that has been divorced has not had a properly functioning family and is not eligible.[46]

It is the past actions of the man that *presently* affects his situation. The past actions of a man who remarries after divorce makes him *presently* be the husband of *more* than one wife. The past actions of the man who divorces his wife presently disqualifies him from leadership.

Divorces normally occur because a man has not managed his household well. Marriage is one of the most probing tests of a man's character and beliefs. Divorce often (but not always) reveals hidden character traits that would further disqualify a man from oversight. Even though the man may not have initiated the divorce it may show that he is unloving, unforgiving, self-willed, harsh, or quick tempered.

46. Derickson, *Notes on Theology*, p. 1087.

Objection—The "one woman man" interpretation emphasizes the positive aspect of this qualification. First Timothy 3:2 contains only positive statements about a man's character. The use of the negative (not) is reserved for other verses. This is the reason that the "husband of one wife" phrase cannot mean "not divorced and remarried."

Answer—The idea that the qualifying verses of First Timothy 3 and Titus 1 are conveniently broken up into positives and negatives is mistaken. The verse numbers are not part of the inspired text. The reasons why Paul was led by the Holy Spirit to use certain negative terms and order the qualifications in this manner are not stated.

First Timothy 3:2 begins with seven so-called positives (defined by the absence of "not" (μη) followed by three so-called negatives (defined by the use of "not" (μη). Next comes one positive "gentle," followed by a true negative "not" (μη) and then somewhat of a negative "no lover of money." "Not" (μη) is not used but the word itself begins the negation "a"). Verse 4 contains two positive statements. Verse 5 is a rhetorical question qualified by a negative "not" (ουκ). Verse 6 contains two negatives "not" (μη). Verse 7 contains a positive and a negative. The rest of First Timothy 3:8–13 (qualifications for deacons) and Titus 1:6–9 (qualifications for elders) is interwoven in similar fashion. There is no clear pattern of positives and negatives.

Simply because qualifications are stated in either a positive or negative manner does not mean that they cannot have opposite implications. A "blameless" man could be interpreted as "*not* open to blame." A "self-controlled" man could be interpreted as "*not* out of control." Conversely, a man who is "*not* violent" and "*not* quick tempered" could be said to be "gentle" or "patient." A man who is "*not* a lover of money" could be interpreted as "content." When this same interpretive principle is applied to the "one wife" phrase the outcome is much the same.

Those who wish to allow divorced and remarried men to serve as elders and deacons often use terms such as "*not* a polygamist," "*not* an adulterer," "*not* flirtatious," "*not* promiscuous," "*not* lustful" as well as other negative phrases. One wonders how they get such negative terminology from such a positive phrase?

In First Timothy 5:9 the phrase "wife of one man" is positive but still contains negative interpretive implications. The woman who may be enrolled on the list of widows could *not* have been divorced and remarried. She could *not* have had two husbands. She also could *not* be under sixty years old.

Objection—All who are allowed into membership should be allowed into leadership.

Answer—The intent of the lists in Timothy and Titus is to exclude the unqualified. The phrase "one woman man" must exclude women. It would certainly exclude polygamists. The phrase "not a new convert" discriminates against new believers. The phrase "able to teach" discriminates against those who are unable to teach. There may be a debate as to the degree of standards but the qualifications are still excluding standards. The lists present specific qualifications of men not merely general qualities.

Calvin writes:

> To sum up, only those are to be chosen who are of sound doctrine and of holy life, not notorious in any fault which might both deprive them of authority and disgrace the ministry (1 Tim. 3:2–3; Titus 1:7–8).[47]

In the Old Testament God had higher marital standards for priests and Levites. The sons of Aaron were not to marry a harlot or a divorced woman (Lev. 21:7). The High priest was not to marry a harlot, divorced woman, or even a widow. He must marry a virgin (Lev. 21:13–15). It is admitted that these standards are not totally analogous with those of elders and deacons but the comparison is made to show that God does require higher standards for those in leadership than for those in the general congregation.

Objection—God Forgives.

Answer—This view could also be called the "it's not fair" interpretation. Since God forgives past sins *it is not fair* to limit those who may serve in oversight.

Eldon Glasscock writes concerning the candidate for leadership:

> If God has forgiven him and made him part of the church, why do Christians hold the past against him.[48]

Glasscock appears to misunderstand the nature of the qualifications for elders and deacons. The qualifications for leadership are given by inspiration of the Holy Spirit (2 Tim. 3:16). It is God who decides who is qualified to shepherd His church. Upholding God's word is not holding a man's past against him. One purpose of this list of qualifications is to exclude certain individuals from leadership. Simply because one has his sins forgiven does not mean that he qualifies for a position of leadership. This

47. John Calvin, *Institutes of the Christian Religion*, Book. 4, ch. 3, Sec. 12.
48. Eldon Glasscock, "'The Husband of One Wife' Requirement in 1 Timothy 3," p. 253.

would mean that all believing men would qualify for leadership because God is always in the continual process of forgiving.

At conversion God forgives all sins past, present, and future because of the work of His Son. The spiritual death penalty is taken away. This does not mean that there are no temporal consequences for sin in this life. A man's alimony payments to his divorced spouse do not cease because he is born again. The familial divisions and relational repercussions that occur because of a divorce may last a life time.

Proponents of this position most often defend a divorce and remarriage that took place before conversion. This is a theologically inconsistent position. A repentant Christian who divorces and remarries is just as forgiven as the non-Christian who divorces and remarries and is later converted. If taken to its logical conclusion an elder who divorces and remarries and then repents is just as forgiven as any other believer. The end result of the "God forgives" position is that any man who divorces and remarries at any stage of his Christian life may serve as an elder. The issue is not whether God forgives divorce and remarriage (He does) or whether divorced and remarried persons can serve God (they can). The real issue is whether a man meets the qualifications for leadership.

An Elder or Deacon must be faithful to one woman at a time.

Most modern proponents of this view follow the teaching of Eldon Glasscock ("'The Husband of One Wife' Requirements in 1 Timothy 3:2," *Bib Sac* 140 [1983]:255). Mr. Glasscock teaches that divorced and remarried persons may serve as elders and deacons as long as they are only legally married to one woman at a time.

Advocates of this position normally favor the expression "one woman kind of man." It is claimed that the elder or deacon must not be flirtatious, promiscuous, or involved in questionable relationships with other women. This is often done with little or no consideration of the number of past marriages of the prospective candidate. It is true that an elder or deacon must not be involved in sinful or questionable relationships. It is not true that this nullifies the God given decree that an elder or deacon must have a life long monogamous commitment to only one woman as his wife.

Proponents of this view normally depreciate the "husband of one wife" translation and prefer the translation "one woman man." The "one woman at a time" position has several weaknesses and virtually no historical proponents. If consistently applied there would be no limit on how many times a man could divorce and remarry. The only thing that would matter is that he is legally married to only one woman at a time. The most common modern application of this teaching is that a man can divorce and remarry one time and still be an elder or deacon but any further marriages are perceived as suspect.

While most defenders of this view would prohibit a polygamist from leadership they have little or no problem in allowing a digamist (one who divorces and remarries). They claim that a man must be faithful to his current wife but fail to see that divorce and remarriage is actually a form of unfaithfulness to his past wife. Furthermore, they do not appear to understand that a divorced and remarried elder may ultimately encourage others to be unfaithful.

The "one woman man" interpretation appears to be unknown before the 20th century. In the past, some have interpreted the phrase as meaning that an elder must be "faithful to his wife" but the addition of the idea of "one at a time" is more than the grammar allows. While neither the newness nor the antiquity of a position is proof of its orthodoxy, the motivation behind this position is certainly suspect. The acceptance of this interpretation appears to be driven by the declining moral status of the evangelical church. As divorce and remarriage have become accepted in the church the acceptance of divorced and remarried men as leaders has also risen.

Derickson writes:

> This is a recent addition to the menu of excuses to skirt Scripture and allow people the freedom to do as they please rather than as the Lord directs.[49]

Most of the defenses of the "one wife at a time" view are actually objections to the no divorce and remarriage view. They have been dealt with in previous chapters.

Conclusion

The lists in First Timothy 3 and Titus 1 are given by God as the minimum requirements of what an elder or deacon *must* be. In some respects they both limit and exclude certain men from serving as elders and deacons.

The emphasis of the "of one wife husband" phrase is on the word "one." This demands that the man who desires oversight remain faithful to one woman throughout his life. A man who is faithful to one wife will not divorce her and marry another. The man who divorces his wife and remarries another is no longer the "husband of *one* wife." This is true even

---

49. Derickson, *Notes on Theology*, p. 1087.

if the divorce and remarriage occurred before his conversion. In the truest biblical sense he is not a "one woman man."

God has high qualifications for elders and deacons. Those who are in leadership are to have impeccable character. The phrase "husband of one wife" prohibits polygamists, adulterers, fornicators, and homosexuals from taking part in local church leadership. It prohibits men who are given over to lust of other women. It would also prohibit men who have committed adultery by divorcing and remarrying. Those who claim an exception, if the divorce and remarriage happened before conversion, need to put forth exegetical proof.

The "husband of one wife" phrase is not one of interpretive exclusivity it is one of interpretive inclusiveness. The prohibition of divorced and remarried men serving as elders and deacons has been held by a majority of Greek exegetes and expositors throughout church history. Although not the only verdict, the prohibition of divorced and remarried men serving as elders and deacons has normally been part of their conclusion. Most commentators have included it as one of the things that would disqualify a man from being a "one wife man." The list normally includes polygamy, concubinage, adultery, fornication, as well as digamy (divorce and remarriage). All of these sins would be excluded by the "husband of one wife" phrase. There are also scholars who would exclude a widower who remarried from serving as an elder or deacon.

The recent rise in the acceptance of divorce and remarriage in the church has also led to a recent rise in the allowance of divorced and remarried men to serve as elders and deacons. Until the 20th century it was difficult to find an exegete or expositor that claimed the "husband of one wife" phrase allowed a man who was divorced and remarried to serve in a position of church leadership. Some, such as Jerome, Theodoret, and Calvin, saw it as a prohibition of the Jewish practice of polygamy but they do not claim that divorced and remarried men could serve as elders.

Beyond being the husband of one wife an elder or deacon must not be open to blame in any area. He must rule his home and children well. If a man does not meet the standards given in First Timothy and Titus he is disqualified from leadership, regardless of other talents, gifts, or qualifications he may have.

Chapter 7

Reducing the Risk

OUTSIDE OF staying single, it may not be possible to eliminate all risk of divorce. It takes a conscious act of the will by two individuals to make a marriage work. It takes the grace of God to daily resist the temptations that seek to tear a marriage apart.

The following guidelines are given to reduce the risk of divorce:

1. A believer should only marry another believer, preferably, someone who has a proven history of walking with the Lord in good times as well as bad.

2. Marry only with parental or guardian approval. Honoring your father and mother is still good biblical advice. Parents may not be able to choose a mate for you, but they generally have one's best interest in mind. They may be able to help discern wrong choices.

3. Marry only with the spiritual blessing of the elders of a local congregation. They are given as shepherds to oversee your soul.

4. Realize marriage is a covenant vow before God, as well as a legal contract before men.

5. Avoid sexual involvement before marriage. Premarital sex produces guilt and builds a barrier of distrust.

6. Marry only a believer with biblical convictions on the permanence of marriage. It is not uncommon for a person who believes divorce and remarriage is an option for others, to exercise it themselves. Knowing that divorce is not an option is a motivating force to work through problems and build a stronger marriage.

7. Fulfill your God ordained roles in the home, local church, and society. God has made men and women for different purposes. Men are to be the primary providers for their families. Though

certain exceptions may arise, this is the normative standard. Men should be spiritual leaders in the home and local assembly. A lazy or unspiritual man can frustrate a woman who desires to be lovingly led.

8. Practice daily forgiveness. If sin arises in the life of your spouse ask God for the grace to forgive them.

9. Make your spouse a priority in your life. Never withhold sex as a form of punishment.

10. Stay spiritually healthy:

   • Daily read the Bible.

   • Fellowship with other believers.

   • Be humble and dependent on the Lord.

11. Keep financial debt to a minimum. Put spiritual and family life before money and career.

12. Do not let the sun go down on your anger.

13. Keep your word.

14. Be involved and "work" on your marriage. Biblical love is an active relationship and decision of the will.

15. Husbands love your wives. Wives submit to your husbands. Pray daily for your spouse.

Summary

I AM AWARE that a significant number of sincere Christians believe it is perfectly all right to divorce and remarry. Sincerity is not the issue; obedience to Christ is.

I claim no infallibility. Some arguments may be stronger than others. I have written for the average Christian, not the scholar. More scholarly men than I have capably dealt with these same issues and come to similar conclusions. Their works are in print for those who wish to read them.

Adultery is a serious charge and is not to be taken lightly. If my conclusions are wrong, I will be judged for being an inaccurate teacher of God's word. If I am right, a significant portion of the evangelical church will need to change its teaching and practice. All the church allows, or disallows, must be based upon God's word.

I stand behind these basic conclusions:

A)   God created marriage to be a lifelong *one flesh* covenant bond between husband and wife.

B)   Sin has distorted God's original plan for marriage.

C)   The Mosaic Law did not establish or approve of divorce. It was already occurring and God gave one law that only prohibited the divorced woman from ever returning to her first husband after she had remarried.

D)   Christ allowed divorce only in the limited case of *porneia*. The "exception clause" is only listed in the Jewish Gospel of Matthew.

E)   The Rabbinic laws of Christ's day compelled a man to divorce a fornicating wife. No such law exists in modern Western society. The Christian is to forgive his brother seventy times seven. The Christian should forgive his spouse in the same manner.

F)   There is no clear teaching in the Bible that the one flesh marriage bond is severed by any thing other than death.

G)   There is no plain mandate in the entire New Testament which teaches that a divorced person may remarry while their spouse is alive.

H)   There are clear statements in the New Testament which call remarriage after divorce adultery.

I)   God completely forgives all sin, including divorce and remarriage. Forgiveness does not necessarily mean freedom from consequences of sin in this life.

J)   The Evangelical Church must not allow more than Christ allowed. The local church should stand ready to forgive those who repent of divorce and remarriage. It must be willing to teach those who seek truth. It must care enough to emotionally and financially support those people who seek to honor Christ by not remarrying.

Appendix

The Heart of God for Reconciliation

One theme of the New Testament is God's heart for reconciliation. The work of Christ is the basis for man's reconciliation to God. The work of Christ is also the basis for reconciliation of families. The work of Christ provides the basis of God's forgiveness of man's sins. It also provides the basis for one spouse to forgive another no matter how grievous the sin. It is forgiveness that is the basis for biblical reconciliation. Divorce, at its root, is the failure of one spouse to forgive the other and be reconciled. Jesus paid the price of blood to see broken families recovered and restored. Jesus is a Healer and a forgiver. He is our example. His will is not for families to be separated and destroyed. The work of forgiveness, healing, and restoration repairs families and brings them back together.

When one spouse sins against the other the heart of God cries out for forgiveness. The heart of God seeks repentance of the sinning spouse but the process may be long and the other spouse should not give up hope that they will repent and return. It is the grace of God that allows for forgiveness. Those who refuse to forgive a wayward spouse are resisting the grace of God and message of the cross. Some believe that the New Testament provides a loophole to divorce a sinning spouse and marry another. To them the work and message of the Cross are not a priority. Those who divorce their spouse and marry another are unaware that their behavior opposes the very heart of God. Their behavior opposes: 1) The healing and restoring work of Christ. 2) The power of the blood to atone for sins. 3) The prayers of children who long to see their families restored. 4) The efforts of others who hope and pray for the restoration of broken families.

Those who seek a divorce from a sinning spouse and seek to marry another advocate that: 1) God is opposed to the future restoration of the marriage. 2) Their spouse does not qualify for God's best, even though purchased by the blood of Christ. 3) They have a moral right to separate what God has joined. 4) Christians should not encourage prayer for the restoration of marriages. 5) Christians should not believe that it is God's will to restore broken marriages. 6) The children of a broken marriage should not pray and hope that their family may be restored.

The message of those who oppose the possibility of reconciliation is a message of destruction to a family. This ultimately weakens both society and the church. God's message is a message of life first to the family and then to the church. The Lord hears and answers prayers. He brings reconciliation to families and the church. Waiting in prayer for a wayward spouse is the ultimate act of overcoming evil with good. In the same way that Christ does not give up on sinners a spouse should not give up hope that they will return and be reconciled. This is the heart of God for reconciliation.

The entire law is summed up in the statement, "You shall love your neighbor as yourself" (Gal. 5:14). "Husbands, love your wives, just as Christ also loved the church and gave Himself for her" (Eph. 5:25). It is doubtful that these words allow for exemptions for a husband to divorce his wife and marry another.

Bibliography

Abbott-Smith, G. *A Manual Greek Lexicon of the New Testament*. Edinburgh: T & T Clark, 1968.

Adams, Jay E. *Marriage, Divorce and Remarriage in the Bible*. Phillipsburg, N.J.: Presbyterian and Reformed, 1980.

Allis, O. T. *Prophecy and the Church*. Phillipsburg, N.J.: Presbyterian and Reformed, 1945.

Ante-Nicene Fathers. Edited by Alexander Roberts and James Donaldson. Peabody, Mass.: Hendrickson, 1994.

Bauer, Walter. *A Greek-English Lexicon of the New Testament*. Translated and revised by W. F. Arndt and F. W. Gingrich. Chicago: University of Chicago, 1952.

Blass, Debrunner, and Funk. *A Greek Grammar of the New Testament*. Chicago: University of Chicago, 1961.

Blomberg, Craig L. "Marriage, Divorce, Remarriage, and Celibacy: An Exegesis of Matthew 19:3–12." *Trinity Journal* n.s. 11 (1990) 161–96.

Boice, James Montgomery. "The Biblical View of Divorce." *Eternity* 21 (December 1970) 9–21.

Bromiley, Geoffrey W. *God and Marriage*. Grand Rapids: Eerdmans, 1980.

Brown, Francis. *The New Brown-Driver-Briggs-Gesenius Hebrew and English Lexicon*. Peabody: Hendrickson, 1979.

Bruce, F. F. *Paul: Apostle of the Heart Set Free*. Grand Rapids: Eerdmans, 1977.

Cairns, Earle E. *Christianity Through the Centuries*. Grand Rapids: Academie, 1981.

Calvin, John. *Institutes of the Christian Religion*. Translated by Henry Beveridge. Grand Rapids: Eerdmans, 1994.

Carson, D. A. *Exegetical Fallacies*. Grand Rapids: Baker, 1996.

Clarke, Adam. *New Testament Commentary* vol. 6b. Albany, OR.: Ages Digital Library, 1996.

Couch, Mal. *Dictionary of Premillennial Theology*. Grand Rapids: Kregel, 1996.

Cragie, Peter C. *The Book of Deuteronomy*. Grand Rapids: Eerdmans, 1976.

Crouzel, Henri. *L' eglise primitive face au divorce du premier au cinquieme siecle*. Paris: Beauchesne, 1971.

Dana, H. E. and Mantey, Julius R. *A Manual Grammar of the Greek New Testament*. Toronto: MacMillan, 1957.

Danby, Herbert. *The Mishnah*. New York: Oxford University Press, 1992.

Derickson, Stanley. *Notes on Theology*. Albany, OR.: Ages Digital Library, 1997.

Durant, Will. *The Story of Civilization: Caesar and Christ*. New York: Simon and Schuster, 1944.

Duty, Guy. *Divorce and Remarriage*. Minneapolis: Bethany Fellowship, 1967.

Edersheim, Alfred. *The Life and Times of Jesus the Messiah*. Peabody: Hendrickson, 1994.

Ellisen, Stanley A. *Divorce and Remarriage in the Church*. Grand Rapids: Zondervan, 1977.

Enns, Paul. *The Moody Handbook of Theology*. Chicago: Moody Press, 1989.

Bibliography

Feinberg, Charles L. *The Minor Prophets.* Chicago: Moody Press, 1976.

Fitzmyer, Joseph A. "The Matthean Divorce Texts and Some New Palestinian Evidence." *Theological Studies* 37 (1976) 197–226.

Gill, John. *Commentary on First Timothy.* Albany, OR.: Ages Digital Library, 1997.

Glasscock, Eldon. "'The Husband of One Wife' Requirement in 1 Timothy 3:2." *Bibliohteca Sacra* 140 (July–September, 1983) 244–258.

Godet, F. L. *The First Epistle to the Corinthians.* Grand Rapids: Zondervan, 1971.

Grosheide, F. W. *Commentary on the First Epistle to the Corinthians.* Grand Rapids: Eerdmans, 1953.

Henry, Matthew. *Commentary on the Whole Bible.* Albany, OR.: Ages Digital Library, 1996.

Heth, William A. "Another look at the Erasmian View of Divorce and Remarriage." *Journal of the Evangelical Theological Society* 25 (1982) 263–72.

Heth, William A. and Wenham, Gordon J. *Jesus and Divorce: The Problem with the Evangelical Consensus.* Nashville: Thomas Nelson, 1985.

Hiebert, D. Edmond. *First Timothy.* Chicago: Moody Press, 1957.

_____. *Titus and Philemon.* Chicago: Moody Press, 1957.

Hodge, Charles. *A Commentary on First and Second Corinthians.* Carlisle: Banner of Truth Trust, 1988.

_____. *A Commentary on Romans.* Carlisle: Banner of Truth Trust, 1989.

Holladay, William L. *A Concise Hebrew and Aramaic Lexicon of the Old Testament.* Grand Rapids: Eerdmans, 1993.

Instone-Brewer, David. *Divorce and Remarriage in the Bible: The Social and Literary Context.* Eerdmans, 2002.

Isaksson, Abel. *Marriage and Ministry in the New Temple.* A Study with Special Reference to Mt. 19:13 [sic]–12 and 1 Cor. 11:3–16. Translated by Neil Tomkinson and Jean Gray. *Acta Seminarii Neotestamentici Upsaliensis* 24 Lund: Gleerup; Copenhagen: Munsgaard, 1965.

Jensen, Joseph. "Does Porneia Mean Fornication? A Critique of Bruce Malina." *Novum Testamentum* 20 (1978) 161–84.

Josephus, Flavius. *The Works of Josephus.* Translated by William Whitson. Peabody, Mass.: Hendrickson, 1993.

Keener, Craig S. *And Marries Another: Divorce and Remarriage in the Teaching of the New Testament.* Peabody, Mass.: Hendrickson, 1991.

Keil, C. F. and Delitzsch, F. *Commentary on the Old Testament.* Grand Rapids: Eerdmans, 1991.

Kent, Homer. *The Pastoral Epistles.* Chicago: Moody Press, 1976.

Kilgallen, John J. "To what are the Matthean Exception-Texts (5, 32 and 19, 9) an Exception?" *Biblica* 61 (1980) 102–5.

Kittel, Gerhard and Friedrich, Gerhard. *Theological Dictionary of the New Testament.* Translated and abridged by Geoffrey W. Bromiley. Grand Rapids: Eerdmans, 1992.

Laney, J. Carl. *The Divorce Myth.* Minneapolis: Bethany Fellowship, 1981.

_____. "Paul and the Permanence of Marriage in First Corinthians 7." *Journal of the Evangelical Society* 25 (1982) 283–94.

Liddell, Henry George and Scott, Robert. *Greek-English Lexicon.* 9th ed. Oxford: Clarendon Press, 1996.

Lowther Clarke, W. K. "The Exception Clause in Matthew." *Theology* 15 (1927) 161–62.

Luther, Martin. *Commentary on Romans.* Translated by Theodore Mueller. Grand Rapids: Kregel, 1976.

MacDonald, William and Farstad, Arthur. *Believers Bible Commentary.* Nashville: Thomas Nelson, 1997.

Malina, Bruce. "Does Porneia Mean Fornication?" *Novum Testamentum* 14 (1972) 10–17.

Mishnah. Translated by Herbert Danby. New York: Oxford University Press, 1992.

Moulton, James and Milligan, George. *The Vocabulary of the Greek New Testament.* Grand Rapids: Eerdmans, 1976.

Mounce, William. *Word Biblical Commentary* vol. 46. Nashville: Thomas Nelson, 2000.

Murray, John. *Divorce.* Phillipsburg, N.J.: Presbyterian and Reformed Publishing Co., 1961.

Nicene and Post-Nicene Fathers. Edited by Philip Schaff, Peabody, Mass.: Hendrickson, 1995.

Olsen, Norskov V. *The New Testament Logia on Divorce: A Study of their interpretation from Erasmus to Milton.* Beitrage zur Geschichte der biblischen Exegese 10. Tubingen: J. C. B. Mohr (Paul Siebeck), 1971.

Osborn, Carroll D. "The Present Indicative in Matthew 19:9." *Restoration Quarterly* 24 (1981) 193–203.

Plummer, Alfred. *An Exegetical Commentary on the Gospel of Matthew.* Grand Rapids: Eerdmans, 1910.

Porter, S. E. and Buchanan, P. "The Logical Structure of Matthew 19:9." *Journal of the Evangelical Theological Society* 34 (1991) 335–39.

Quesnell, Quentin. "Made themselves Eunuchs for the Kingdom of Heaven (Mt. 19, 12)." *Catholic Biblical Quarterly* 30 (1968) 335–58.

Robertson, A. T. *Word Pictures in the New Testament.* Grand Rapids: Baker, 1930.

_____. *A Grammar of the Greek New Testament in the Light of Historical Research.* Nashville, Tenn.: Broadman Press, 1934.

Robertson, A. and Plummer, A. *First Epistle of Saint Paul to the Corinthians.* Edinburgh: T & T Clark, 1994.

Ryrie, Charles C. "Biblical Teaching on Divorce and Remarriage." *Grace Theological Journal* 3 (1982) 177–92.

_____. Basic Theology. Wheaton: Victor, 1994.

Saucy, Robert L. "The Husband of One Wife." *Bibliotheca Sacra* 131 (1974) 229–40.

Schaff, Philip. *The Creeds of Christendom.* Grand Rapids: Baker, 1993.

Straus, Lehman. *The Permanency of the Marriage Relationship.* n.a.

Thayer, Joseph H. *Greek-English Lexicon of the New Testament.* Grand Rapids: Zondervan, 1981.

Trepp, Leo. *The Complete Book of Jewish Observance.* New York: Simon and Schuster, 1980.

Vawter, Bruce. "The Divorce Clauses in Mt 5:32 and 19:9." *Catholic Biblical Quarterly* 16 (1954): 155–67.

Vincent, Marvin. *Word Studies in the New Testament.* McLean, VA.: Mac Donald Publishing, n.a.

Vine, W. E. *An Expository Dictionary of New Testament Words.* Nashville: Thomas Nelson, 1968.

Walvoord, John F. and Zuck, Roy B. *The Bible Knowledge Commentary.* Wheaton: Victor Books, 1983.

Wenham, Gordon J. "The Biblical View of Marriage and Divorce 3-New Testament Teachings." *Third Way,* (1977) 7–9.

_____. "The Syntax of Matthew 19.9." *Journal for the Study of the New Testament* 28 (1986) 17–23.

Wesley, John. *Notes on First Timothy*. Albany, OR.: Ages Digital Library, 1996.

Westbrook, Raymond. "Prohibition of the Restoration of Marriage in Deuteronomy 24:1–4." In *Studies in Bible* 1986, ed. S. Japhet, p. 387–405. *Scripta Hierosolymitana* 31. Jerusalem: Magnes, 1986.

White, Newport. "The First and Second Epistles to Timothy and Titus." In *The Expositors Greek Testament*, 83–202. Peabody, Mass.: Hendrickson, 2002.

Wuest, Kenneth. *The Pastoral Epistles*. Grand Rapids: Eerdmans, 1960.

Yamauchi, Edwin M. "Cultural Aspects of Marriage in the Ancient World." *Bibliotheca Sacra* 135 (1978) 241–52.

www.ingramcontent.com/pod-product-compliance
Lightning Source LLC
Chambersburg PA
CBHW060344100426

42812CB00003B/1120